T0086776

AIRLINE HIGHWAY

AIRLINE HIGHWAY

⊰ A PLAY ⊱

LISA D'AMOUR

NORTHWESTERN UNIVERSITY PRESS

EVANSTON, ILLINOIS

Northwestern University Press
www.nupress.northwestern.edu

Copyright © 2015 by Lisa D'Amour. Published 2015 by Northwestern University Press. All rights reserved.

Printed in the United States of America

10 9 8 7 6 5 4 3 2

Professionals and amateurs are hereby warned that this material, being fully protected under the Copyright Laws of the United States of America and all other countries of the copyright union, is subject to a royalty. All rights, including, but not limited to, professional, amateur, recording, motion picture, recitation, lecturing, public reading, radio and television broadcasting, and the rights of translation into foreign language, are strictly reserved. All inquiries regarding performance rights for this play should be addressed to Antje Oegel, AO International, aoegel@aoegelinternational .com; (001) 773-754-7628.

SPECIAL NOTE ON SONGS AND RECORDINGS
For performance of copyrighted songs, arrangements, or recordings mentioned in the play, the permission of the copyright owner(s) must be obtained. Other songs, arrangements, or recordings may be substituted provided permission from the copyright owner(s) of such songs, arrangements, or recordings is obtained; or songs, arrangements, or recordings in the public domain may be substituted.

The poetry that Francis quotes in the play is from two poets with New Orleans roots, John Sinclair and Daniel Kerwick, and is used with permission.

ISBN 978-0-8101-3288-7 (paper)

Library of Congress Cataloging-in-Publication data are available from the Library of Congress.

♾ The paper used in this publication meets the minimum requirements of the American National Standard for Information Sciences—Permanence of Paper for Printed Library Materials, ANSI Z39.48-1992.

CONTENTS

PRODUCTION HISTORY

Airline Highway, by Lisa D'Amour, received its world premiere on December 14, 2014, at Steppenwolf Theatre in Chicago (Martha Lavey, Artistic Director, and David Hawkanson, Executive Director). It was directed by Joe Mantello, with scenic design by Scott Pask, costume design by David Zinn, lighting design by Japhy Weideman, and original music and sound design by Fitz Patton. The Steppenwolf production was stage managed by Malcolm Ewen. The production moved to Manhattan Theatre Club's Samuel J. Friedman Theatre for a Broadway run in April 2015, and was stage managed by Diane Di Vita. *Airline Highway* was commissioned and developed by Steppenwolf with support from the Andrew W. Mellon Foundation.

The cast of the Chicago production was as follows:

Terry . . . . Tim Edward Rhoze
Krista . . . . Caroline Neff
Wayne . . . . Scott Jaeck
Sissy Na Na . . . . K. Todd Freeman
Francis . . . . Gordon Joseph Weiss
Tanya . . . . Kate Buddeke
Bait Boy . . . . Stephen Louis Grush
Zoe . . . . Carolyn Braver
Miss Ruby . . . . Judith Roberts
Ensemble . . . . Robert Breuler, Chris Daley, Terry Hamilton,
Toni Martin, Brenann Stacker, and Jacqueline Williams

For the Broadway run, the cast changed as follows:

Francis. . . . . Ken Marks
Tanya . . . . Julie White
Bait Boy . . . . Joe Tippett

Ensemble . . . . Todd D'Amour, Shannon Eagen, Venida Evans,
Joe Forbrich, Lisa Hendrix, and Sekou Laidlow

AUTHOR'S NOTE

The action of the play takes place over the course of one day, in which the characters plan and throw a party. As much as possible there should be a sense of simultaneous and interlocking conversations.

To capture the commotion onstage, I've used several techniques in this printed edition. When dialogue appears in columns, the layout gives a rough indication of how conversations overlap. This overlap can be adjusted to suit different productions; shown here is the pacing we arrived at in order to allow the audience to hear important details while still experiencing the conversational flow.

Sometimes a slash (/) is used to indicate the point at which the next character should begin speaking. Slashes only apply within the column in which they occur.

Even when no columns are present and we seem to cut back and forth between conversations, there should still be a sense of simultaneity, of many conversations happening at once at a party.

This play is set in May 2014 in New Orleans. I'm a fifth-generation New Orleanean. We moved here, to my mother's hometown, when I was nine. I was away for many of my post-college years, rooted back here by age forty. As New Orleans approaches the tenth year after Katrina, the city feels caught between preserving a culture created pre-Internet (in an environment that often felt hermetically sealed and resistant to change) and embracing an influx of post-Katrina money, residents, and ideas. New Orleans, like most American cities, is becoming a more expensive place to live and play. There is a growing fear that its rituals and traditions, created by people of many races and income brackets, will be harder to sustain as the city gets taken over by "outside money." It's a heated, city-wide conversation; the characters in this play feel overwhelmed by it, or perhaps not empowered to be a part of it. Whatever the case may be, know that the stress of a home disappearing, a way of life evaporating, hovers over this party in the midst of all the celebration.

Thanks to Martha Lavey and Steppenwolf Theatre for commissioning and producing the premiere of the play, to Lynn Meadow and Manhattan Theatre Club for moving the play to the Samuel J. Friedman Theatre in New York, to Joe Mantello for his mentorship and expert direction of both productions, and to my family in New Orleans: Tay, Gene, Chris, Todd, Landen, Jolie, and the many circles of relatives that spiral out from there. Thanks also to my agent, Antje Oegel, to my husband, Brendan Connelly, and to my New Orleans theater colleagues, especially ArtSpot Productions and Mondo Bizarro.

AIRLINE HIGHWAY

CHARACTERS

TERRY—African American, could be any age between forty-five and fifty-five. Originally from the country, New Iberia, Louisiana, but he has been in NOLA for quite some time—mostly to get away from the crowd he ran with in the country, who were up to no good. He is a handyman and has the bad habit of ingratiating himself to people with money in order to get work from them—and then really wanting to impress them. And then getting overwhelmed and failing to do the job well and then, often, running. He cycles back to the Hummingbird every couple of months, after working for different people there and then screwing up. He has carried a torch for Krista for a few years now, and you know, maybe they did fool around a little once, at sunrise, at the end of one of the Hummingbird parking lot parties, when they were both a little toasted. But have they talked about it since? Of course not.

KRISTA—White, early thirties, a stripper at Babe's on Bourbon Street. A gentle soul who turns rabid, however, when she feels like she is being threatened or when she gets too close to someone. Always looking for people to take care of her, but pushes them away once they do. Grew up in a small town in northern Mississippi before moving to Mobile, Alabama, and then Slidell, Louisiana.

WAYNE—White, early sixties. Manager of the Hummingbird Hotel—he lives in a small apartment above the front office. Of old-school, working-class, Irish-German-NOLA descent. Potbelly. The sweetest man on Airline Highway, too sweet, actually, way too happy to just be hanging out with interesting people, which is why he has not become anything other than the manager of the Hummingbird Hotel. Divorced some time ago. No kids.

MAN ONE—White. A john visiting Tanya in her room at the Hummingbird.

SISSY NA NA—Black. More specifically, a New Orleans blend of Afro-Caribbean blood. Midforties. Trans bartender and karaoke wrangler at the Cat's Meow on Bourbon Street. No operations or hormones— she just dresses to reflect who she is. Though not without her demons, at the end of the day Sissy may be the most functional of all these lovable fools. She's got no patience for fooling around, she gets the job *done*. Maybe, probably, she gets other people's jobs done way more than she takes care of her own shit, you know? She is seduced by the potential of a joyful moment, of people having *fun* and letting their guard down. This is why she has a special kind of love for her profession, and yes, she does consider karaoke wrangling a profession, shut up.

MAN TWO—White. Another john visiting Tanya in her room.

FRANCIS—White, midfifties. The mind, creativity, and energy of a thirty-year-old, but the grizzly beard, worn face, and watery eyes of a much older, lifelong (happy) social drinker. A true poet, child of the Beats, he's been scribbling out poems for years, with deep roots in the New Orleans poetry scene. A man-about-town, at all the right parties, a little too old for certain scenes, but he's always there, always on the move, always taking it all in.

SHADY CHARACTER ONE—Male, between twenty and forty years old. One of a group of people living temporarily in the room at the Hummingbird Hotel known as the Problem Room. The characters who inhabit the Problem Room should be a mix of races, definitely not all white or all black.

TANYA—White, sixty-two. She's an old-school hooker, been in and out of the business for many years, sometimes bartending, a bit of exotic dancing in the early days, not working at all for the year ten years ago when she was married to the rich banker from California. Tried for a while to run her own business giving in-home facials—lost a lot of money on that one. So for the past few years, she has been back at it, working out of the Hummingbird, servicing quite a few regular, mature clients. She can handle alcohol, but she *can* turn into a crazy person when it comes to pain pills.

SHADY CHARACTER TWO—Female, between twenty and forty years old. Living temporarily in the Problem Room.

SHADY CHARACTER THREE—Male, between twenty and forty years old. A drug dealer living temporarily in the Problem Room.

NURSE'S AIDE—Black female, more than fifty-five years old. Hospice worker who visits Miss Ruby.

BAIT BOY—White, midthirties. He has been a bartender, bouncer, barker outside strip joints, karaoke wrangler, waiter, and street musician (keyboard), all in the Quarter. Long romantic history with Krista. Currently living "the straight life" in Atlanta with an older woman, maybe in her early fifties. Has worked hard these past few years to "pass" as an educated suburban guy.

ZOE—White, sixteen. Bait Boy's stepdaughter. She's a junior at the magnet high school in Atlanta—honors track. Learns fast, too fast—her book smarts run ahead of her emotional maturity. She does not realize how little she has lived.

PARTY GUESTS—Guests at Miss Ruby's party, an assortment of ages and races. The minimum is seven guests, who double as other characters; more can be added. However many are on stage, the feeling is that Miss Ruby's party is large and joyful.

JUDGE HARMON—White, seventies, a friend of Miss Ruby's.

MISS RUBY—Can be cast as white or black. Let's say she's eighty-five. Dying (literally dying), infamous Bourbon Street burlesque performer; had a club on Bourbon Street for years. Kind of the "mama" of Bourbon Street, she has had many ups and downs. At her core a brilliant businesswoman and show person, and also a woman ahead of her time when it comes to thinking about women's bodies, sex, and objectification. If she had been born later, she might have been a performance artist, the belle of the art world. Instead she is the Belle of Bourbon Street, destined to be loved by a few and then forgotten.

PLACE

The Hummingbird Hotel on Airline Highway, New Orleans, Louisiana.

TIME

The first weekend of May, 2014.

ACT 1

SCENE 1

[*The lights rise at as close to the dawn's pace as can be managed in a theater. It is five forty-five in the morning in the parking lot of the Hummingbird, a hotel on Airline Highway on the northwestern edge of New Orleans just before it turns into Metairie. It is one of those old-school hotels from maybe the forties, with an old neon sign portraying a big blue and yellow hummingbird holding a flower in its mouth and the words "The Hummingbird" underneath it.*

The hotel office is visible downstage right, with floor to ceiling glass windows, and the U-shaped hotel, with two floors of rooms, opening up onto a shared parking lot. There is a black, rusted wrought-iron rail along the second floor walkway. There is one abandoned car in the lot—maybe it is up on cinder blocks. A gutter pipe hangs down stage left, near the office, rusted, maybe with a green vine that has grown all the way up it.

The hotel, as you might imagine, has seen better days, back when it was a modern hotel with a fresh coat of hummingbird-pink paint on Airline Highway, the main thoroughfare in and out of New Orleans that took you straight to Baton Rouge.

Now it is a dirty beige—remnants of a paint job about fifteen years ago when it was painted an awkward shade of yellow. Some doors have numbers, some don't. While the hotel has occasional out of town guests, most of the people in the rooms work in the service industry in the French Quarter—bartenders, bouncers, dishwashers, karaoke DJs, strippers, and so on.

The light is changing slowly from purple to pink to something approaching day. In the middle of that light is TERRY, *who is nobody, really, hanging out in his spot: perhaps on the top walkway, or on the middle part of the stairs, watching the traffic go by on Airline Highway, smoking a cigarette.*

In these opening moments, perhaps just prior to curtain and just after, several guests at the Hummingbird are seen emerging and doing their thing. Perhaps getting ice, or a Coke from the machine, or walking out of the parking lot to catch the bus. At least one of these guests is SHADY CHARACTER ONE, *who emerges from what will come to be known as the Problem Room: a room filled with too many people, mostly young, but maybe a couple old; it's smoky in there and there's loud music playing. There's trouble in there.*

These figures walk by TERRY *but do not faze him. He smokes and watches the world go by. For a moment the stage is quiet. A few birds, the sun emerging.*

Then the whirr of cars driving by again, and the sound of a bus stopping: air brakes, the door opening, people getting off the bus.

TERRY *times it perfectly so that he finishes his cigarette, crushes it under his heel, and pushes it off the side of the balcony before* KRISTA *enters—dressed in sweatpants and an oversized hoodie. She wears heavy makeup and carries a gym bag.*]

KRISTA: You smoking?

TERRY: No ma'am.

KRISTA: I walk up there, I'm going to smell smoke on you?

TERRY: Yes ma'am, you will. Because I wash dishes at a bar. And everybody smokes there. And I don't have money for laundry. So I haven't washed clothes in two weeks.

[KRISTA *reaches under her hoodie and starts taking off her bra, pulling it out from the sleeves of her hoodie.*]

KRISTA: Fair enough. Don't smoke.

TERRY: I wouldn't do that to you.

KRISTA: It's not me I'm worried about.

TERRY: I stopped smoking. You stop stripping.

KRISTA: It's only temporary.

TERRY: How many years temporary?

KRISTA: And I'm damn good at it. Fuck you . . .

[WAYNE *shuffles into the interior space of the lobby in his pj's and slippers to put coffee on. He is barely awake, starts the coffee.*]

[*Upstairs, a door opens and* MAN ONE, *maybe fifty, wearing sunglasses and dressed in pants and a shirt with a button-down collar, leaves a room—*TANYA's *room.* KRISTA *says "good morning" quietly,* TERRY *kind of nods hello.* MAN ONE *just walks away. Another door opens, and* SISSY NA NA *walks out in her bathrobe and platform boots, tall, brown-skinned, strikingly lean body, hair in a hairnet or maybe tied up with a bandana, no makeup, but a scarf around her neck. She says the following plainly.*]

SISSY NA NA: Morning, ho's. Tanya needs my rubbing alcohol. Thinks she's got an ear infucktion.

KRISTA [*indicating the door* SISSY NA NA *came out of*]: You've been in there all night?

SISSY NA NA: Since I got off work, 'round three.

TERRY: How's Miss Ruby doing in there?

SISSY NA NA: Not good. She keeps calling me Charlie.

KRISTA: Who's Charlie?

TERRY [*to* KRISTA]: Her son who died in Iraq.

SISSY NA NA: Can't you see the resemblance?

[SISSY NA NA *does a silly girlie pose.*]

KRISTA: Oh. Well, it's dark in there. We should open the blinds today.

SISSY NA NA: The light hurts her eyes.

[SISSY NA NA *knocks on* TANYA's *door.*]

Tanya. Tanya. Tanya. Tanya. Tanya.

[*The door opens a crack.*]

Here.

[SISSY NA NA *passes the rubbing alcohol through the doorway. And the door closes.* SISSY NA NA *speaks to* TERRY.]

You got a cigarette?

TERRY: No.

SISSY NA NA: Really?

TERRY: I'm clean.

[SISSY NA NA *gives* TERRY *a big sniff.*]

SISSY NA NA [*calling his bluff*]: Hmph.

[SISSY NA NA *goes back to her room.* MAN TWO, *also dressed in generic white-guy slightly businessy clothes, walks into the parking lot, looks at a little piece of paper, and heads to* TANYA's *room.* WAYNE *pokes his head out of the office. He speaks loudly, not quite yelling.*]

WAYNE: Coffee.

[MAN TWO, *in the midst of going up the steps, is startled.*]

MAN TWO: What?

KRISTA: Nothing, he's just letting us know coffee.

MAN TWO: Oh, uh.

TERRY: It's cool.

MAN TWO: Oh.

[*Maybe a slightly awkward moment here where* MAN TWO *hesitates, then goes to* TANYA's *room and is let in.*]

KRISTA [*to* TERRY]: Why are you here so early?

TERRY: Gonna go see if Mr. Wayne will pay me to fix those gutter pipes.

KRISTA: Those gutter pipes have been hanging like that since forever.

TERRY: They need to be fixed.

KRISTA: I guess.

TERRY: It's bad for the foundation—the water leaks down and the foundation will crack.

KRISTA: How you gonna fix that gutter pipe, Terry? / If you start hammering on it, it's gonna bust into a billion pieces . . .

TERRY: I'm gonna tack it back up with some nice nails and some wire—I know how to fix a gutter pipe.

[FRANCIS *rides up on a sturdy bike that he probably made himself. He is wearing a helmet that perhaps drops down over part of his face, like a biker or motorcycle helmet he has transformed into a mask. It is decorated with tin foil, Mardi Gras beads, doubloons, and glitter. In this moment, he quotes the poet John Sinclair; elsewhere, Daniel Kerwick . . .*]

FRANCIS:
  Ashes to ashes,
  dirt to dirt,
  love, work & suffer
  is our sentence here on earth

  & ain't nobody
  getting out of here alive—

  Happy Jazz Fest, people!

[KRISTA *does fake little poetry-scene snaps, and* FRANCIS *laughs a delicious, high-pitched "I'm still buzzed and life is beautiful" laugh.*]

FRANCIS: He make coffee yet?

KRISTA: Yeah.

FRANCIS: Thank frikken god. I gotta be over at work in, like, two
    hours and—hold on—

[FRANCIS *moves to the door for the coffee.*]

    You want some?

KRISTA: Sure.

[FRANCIS *goes in. There is a moment of silence between* TERRY *and*
KRISTA. *It is as if they hear the day dawning.*]

TERRY: Do you ever sleep?

KRISTA: Sure I sleep. But I'm saving up money to take a trip home to
    Alabama to see my family, so I'm not sleeping right now.

[*Maybe she shoots the bird at him.*]

    Did Wayne rent my room yet?

TERRY: Not yet.

KRISTA [*kind of under her breath*]: Asshole.

[*A moment, as the sun continues to rise.*]

[FRANCIS *comes back out with two paper cups of coffee. He hands*
KRISTA *her coffee when he says "here."*]

FRANCIS: Man, last night, the Soul Rebels—
    forget about it!
    It was like New Orleans in 1989—
    here—
    back when you could still be a dirty motherfucker
    smoking in bars and eat big fat burgers

without worrying where the meat came from.
They rolled into Sydney's at like one A.M.—
they had just played some Bar Mitzvah, Bat Mitzvah, whatever—
and were flying high as frikken Goodyear blimps,
taking over the middle of the bar,
James *blasting* his trumpet and sweating all over some
tourist from Michigan,
Timmy with his sax all up under some woman's skirt
blowing away—she's laughin'!
And then in walks Uncle Sherell,
in his sequined jacket, with two sorority girls,
one under each arm.
Just like dirty dancing or whatever,
I mean he's seventy-eight—let him have his fun!

TERRY: Francis, you think you got that five spot you owe me?

FRANCIS: Yeah, sure I got it.

[FRANCIS *makes no move to give it to* TERRY.]

Jazz Fest is still Jazz Fest, man, you gotta love it.
I mean not the Fest itself—
fuck that and their seventy-five-dollar tickets,
Kid Rock on the "Coors Light" stage.
The real Fest is on the edges . . .
The center will not motherfucking hold.
Because tourists don't want a Coyote Ugly chain / training wheel
strip joint,
they don't want a parade *inside* the convention center,
sponsored by Coke
They want some dirty shit to happen,
authentic top-shelf shit,
the stuff they keep under the counter,
ya gotta ask for it.

Sip it in the back room with a one-eyed banjo player named
Biff—
that's what people want . . .

You should come with me, Krista,
Beah's having a brunch
in just a couple hours—
it's gonna be a blast . . .

KRISTA: I thought you had to work.

FRANCIS: Yeah, but I was going to stop by on my *way* to work.
    I mean, what's the rush? Come on . . .

KRISTA: No. Miss Ruby's funeral is today. It's gonna be nice.

[MAN TWO *leaves* TANYA's *room, perhaps tucking in his shirt. He
moves down the stairs.*]

    [*Under her breath*] That was fast.

[FRANCIS, TERRY, *and* KRISTA *crack up;* MAN TWO *kind of stops and
looks at them.*]

TERRY: It's okay, man, you're good, you're good.

FRANCIS: Don't listen to them, happy Jazz Fest / man.

TERRY: Happy Jazz Fest!

[*They keep laughing as* MAN TWO *kind of scurries away.*]

FRANCIS: You know Bait Boy's coming back for the party today?

[KRISTA *panics but tries her best to contain it.*]

KRISTA: No.

FRANCIS: Yes.

KRISTA: No, he's not; he lives in Atlanta.

[WAYNE *comes out and lights a cigarette.*]

WAYNE: Good morning, my beauties.

FRANCIS: Yeah, he does, but he is coming down with his daughter.

KRISTA [*blanching*]: Daughter?

FRANCIS: No, no, stepdaughter. That chick he wound up with, you know that rich cougar he met at a bar, she's got a daughter from another marriage.

KRISTA: Another marriage? They're married?

[SISSY NA NA *enters from her room carrying a yogurt and a plastic spoon.*]

SISSY NA NA: Child, I shoulda gone to nursing school, I woulda been the star.

FRANCIS: Yeah, he's bringing her down—the stepdaughter, for some school thing or something . . .

TERRY: Hey, Mr. Wayne, you need me to fix the gutters?

WAYNE: Don't call me Mr. Wayne, Terry.

TERRY: I can't help it. You need me to fix the gutters?

WAYNE [*looking up at the gutter pipes*]: Well . . .

[*Nondominant line*]
Let me think about it . . .

KRISTA: How do you know all this?

FRANCIS: Well, he wrote me a letter to pay me back the five frikken hundred dollars he's been owing me for like eight years, and he told me about his cougar wife and step-daughter in the letter. And then he called Sissy because Sissy left him a message about the party.

KRISTA [*to* SISSY NA NA]: Sissy, he called you?

SISSY NA NA: Who?

KRISTA: Bait Boy.

SISSY NA NA: Oh yeah, I told you.

KRISTA: You didn't tell me.

SISSY NA NA: I didn't tell you? I told you. I called Bait Boy to tell him about / the funeral.

FRANCIS: She called him to tell him about the funeral.

KRISTA [*to* SISSY NA NA]: Well, why didn't you . . . why didn't you ask me, I woulda called him.

SISSY NA NA: You ain't got his number. And Miss Ruby asked for him.

KRISTA: I just—I wish . . . I can't—oh never mind, it's fine. I just—

I wish you would have warned me is all.

[FRANCIS *and* SISSY NA NA *feel just a little bit sad for* KRISTA. *Perhaps some look or gesture is exchanged between* FRANCIS *and* SISSY NA NA.]

TERRY: I can tack it back up with some nice nails and some wire . . .

WAYNE: It does really look bad, doesn't it?

TERRY: And if the water just flows down under the pavement, it's gonna affect your foundation.

WAYNE: Oh, I bet the foundation is shot anyway, I mean this hotel is built on soup.

TERRY: I'll do it for a hundred dollars—who else is going to do that job for a hundred dollars?

SISSY NA NA: I mean I'm not *happy* he's coming.

FRANCIS: I'm ambivalent.

WAYNE: I don't know, I gotta ask the owners.

TERRY: Surprise the owners!
Think about the whaddaya
call it—curb appeal. I mean
they're putting in that . . .
that—

[TERRY *points across the street.*]

WAYNE: *Costco.* It's gonna be a
Costco.

TERRY: Gonna be a big shiny
Costco—tore down two
pawnshops and a car wash to
put up that Costco. The owners gonna want the Hum-
mingbird to look *classy.*

WAYNE: Gonna take a lot more
than a gutter pipe.

[WAYNE *smokes, joins the other
convo.*]

Bait Boy's hilarious. I wonder
what that nut's up to . . .

SISSY NA NA: Come on now, don't
worry—

FRANCIS: Don't worry about
frikken Bait Boy—

KRISTA: Francis, do I look fat?

FRANCIS: You're wearing a
hoodie.

KRISTA: I know, but some girls
look skinny in a hoodie.

FRANCIS: I hate skinny girls.

KRISTA: I know, but do I look fat?

[TERRY *tries to push for work again.*]

TERRY: Mr. Wayne—

WAYNE: So, how's quitting smoking going, Terry?

TERRY: Okay, it's going okay. It's been two weeks.

WAYNE: I admire you, Terry. I can't quit to save my life. One time I quit for three days and I woke up one morning with a whole pile of butts next to my bed—I had smoked half a pack in my sleep.

TERRY: It's hard.

WAYNE: Yep.

FRANCIS: Baby, you are the finest gal on Airline Highway.

KRISTA: Shut up!

SISSY NA NA: Hey, what about me?

[FRANCIS *is cracking up.*]

[SHADY CHARACTER TWO *comes out of the Problem Room.*]

SISSY NA NA: Hey, hey, are you the registered guest in that room?

[SHADY CHARACTER TWO *shoots the bird, walks away.*]

[*To* SISSY NA NA] Forget it Sissy, they're paid up, they paid for the whole week.

Sissy, I got pressure on to keep these rooms filled, it hasn't been a problem, they've been no trouble. Sissy, forget about it, okay?

I said are you the registered guest—Wayne, Wayne, stop that girl, I mean how many people are in that room, do you know what they are doing in that room? I don't care that they are paid up, that is a *Problem Room* that is a disaster waiting to happen / and it is your responsibility—okay fine, you're in charge here, I got my own fish to fry, okay, okay.

FRANCIS [*quoting John Sinclair*]: And the new poetry would burn itself down to one word, and the poets would say it and then everybody would be a poet. And the word would burn itself into everybody's body meat and men would hold hands and smile . . .

TERRY: So can I fix it?

WAYNE: Can you fix it today?

TERRY: Sure, I can fix it today. I could really use the help.

My son over in Eunice, he, he got hit by a car.

WAYNE: I heard about that, Terry.

TERRY: He's doing okay, but he's still in the hospital and I'm trying to get together the money to go see him—

WAYNE: Go ahead, Terry.

TERRY: Thank you, Mr. Wayne, thank you.

[KRISTA *shakes out her hair, nervous about the* BAIT BOY *news.* SISSY NA NA *has gone into her room or maybe a storage closet? Continuing to prep for the party.*]

FRANCIS [*to* KRISTA]: You need some sleep.

[KRISTA *kind of waves him off.*]

[FRANCIS *walks over behind* KRISTA *and rubs her shoulders.*]

WAYNE: Stop calling me that!

[WAYNE *goes inside, gets money out of the till, comes back.*]

Here's fifty dollars for supplies. Bring me receipts and we'll settle up.

TERRY: I'm going now, it'll be done by noon, I bet. If not noon, then one P.M.

WAYNE: Fine . . . good . . . fantabulous . . .

KRISTA: Get off me, Francis, you smell like beer.

[FRANCIS *kind of shrugs, like, "So?"*]

[TERRY *walks toward the street, out of sight.* TANYA *comes out of her room, effortlessly joining the conversation.*]

SISSY NA NA: All us miserable rug rats gotta step up for Miss Ruby.

TANYA: Absolutely. She wanted a funeral before she was dead, and we are gonna give it to her.

FRANCIS: Why do we gotta wait until we're in the coffin for people to say nice things about us?

WAYNE: Yeah, like maybe if those people said those things earlier, we'd live longer.

KRISTA: Who wants to live longer?

SISSY NA NA AND FRANCIS: Krista . . .

[WAYNE *goes into the lobby and up the inside stairs.*]

TANYA: Anyway, I've got a list for us. Shit, hold on, let me get my glasses.

[TANYA *goes back into her room.*]

FRANCIS: What time is it?

SISSY NA NA: It was six A.M. like ten minutes ago.

FRANCIS: Shit, I gotta get going.

[FRANCIS *makes absolutely no move to go.* SISSY NA NA *eats her yogurt and rants.*]

SISSY NA NA: Fuck all them short-dicked doe-eyed tight-lipped tourists from Minnesota. What is there, a convention of polite-ass Minnesotans in town? Michigan, Minnesota, whatever, up there, in that general area . . .

I mean, I'm all like, hello, *hello,* can I help you, and they're like [*speaking with a nasal accent*] "Um, do you have a menu?" "Excuse me, thanks, do you have any nonalcoholic beer other than O'Doul's?" And I'm like, bitch, you're lucky we have O'Doul's! "Excuse me, ma'am, can we take our beers onto the street?" And it's like sometimes I think people don't have *eyes*—can't they see *everybody* has their beers in go cups on the street? And

FRANCIS: Michigan. It's Michigan. It's some kind of music appreciation group from Michigan. I know, they're like kindergarteners, they need to be tied together with yarn . . .

[FRANCIS *is cracking up.*]

they are just—I mean, it's like
someone injected a cloud into
their head, like the doctor injected a cloud into their head
when they were born, so
that now they are all, like—
Ooooooh, oooookaaaaay,
weeeellll, that's straaaaange,
but I guesssssss soooo.

KRISTA: They're good tippers, at least, the men from Michigan. I think
it makes them feel better about being in a titty bar.

[TANYA *comes back out with her list, wearing her reading glasses.*]

TANYA: All right, so Francis, three bags of tortilla chips.

FRANCIS: Three bags! / We don't need three bags! You people eat too
much . . .

TANYA: Party-sized bags—*yes we do,* I have thrown a lot of parties in
my life, I know what we need.

FRANCIS: All right, but I'm going to be a little late.

TANYA: That's all right, so will everybody. Krista, you bring salsa, and
also can you swing paper cups?

KRISTA: You told me yesterday, I brought some from the club.

TANYA: Good girl. Sissy, you're gonna do a vegetable platter? With
ranch?

SISSY NA NA: You still going to the store today?

TANYA: Yeah.

SISSY NA NA: Okay, I'll ride with you, Rouses has a good one.

TANYA: Wayne. *Wayne!*

[WAYNE *pokes his head out of an upstairs window above the office.*]

WAYNE: *What?!*

FRANCIS: He's taking a shit.

KRISTA: No he's not.

FRANCIS: Yes he is.

TANYA [*yelling to* WAYNE]: You're bringing rolls for the cold cuts?

WAYNE: Yeah, and also I got a watermelon.

KRISTA: No he's—

TANYA: Wayne, I love you.

WAYNE: Great, now can I finish my morning crap in peace?

FRANCIS: Told you.

[WAYNE *closes the window.*]

TANYA: Has anybody seen Terry?

KRISTA: He's at the hardware store.

TANYA: He said he could get a keg.

KRISTA: He did?

TANYA: He said he could get a keg donated.

KRISTA: But how would he get it here?

TANYA: I don't know, he said he would.

KRISTA [*skeptically*]: All right.

TANYA: He'll come through. I asked him about it twice, and he said definitely. I'm getting cold cuts and condiments and Miss Ruby's niece is going to bring a sheet cake and the girls from Ruby's old club are going to bring salad and some Zapp's.

FRANCIS: What time again?

TANYA: Two o'clock.

FRANCIS: Okay, I'll be here like three thirty.

TANYA: What else do you have to do?

FRANCIS: I've got work. And I'm going to stop by Beah's brunch.

TANYA: Is there coffee?

KRISTA: Yeah.

[TANYA *goes to get some.*]

SISSY NA NA: I'm thinking about shaving my head.

KRISTA: I did that once.

SISSY NA NA: I mean I'm always in a wig anyway. And this hair is *heavy*. It gets all sweaty up under there. And then it gets itchy. And then it, like, ooooonnnne drip starts to drip down right here. Ooh! Give me the chills.

[TANYA *comes out with a cup of coffee.*]

If I shaved it all off it would be easy, and smooth. Like Tanya's hoo-ha, back in the day.

TANYA [*kind of showing off her lady goods*]: Hey! It's still in fighting form, I'll have you know.

SISSY NA NA: Please, no!

KRISTA: Or a Buddhist.

TANYA: What?

KRISTA: If Sissy shaved her head. Like a Buddhist.

SISSY NA NA [*kind of shaking her butt and bouncing into her room, which is next door to* MISS RUBY's *room*]: Booty booty booty booty booty booty booty booty.

[FRANCIS *gets on his bike, putting on his helmet.*]

FRANCIS: Later, kids.

TANYA: Bye Frannie. Bring the chips by early if you can!

[FRANCIS *says "Yep!" as he rides off.* TANYA *takes a sip of her coffee. It's getting hot outside.* TANYA *fans herself.*]

Whoo, hot!

KRISTA: Did you know Bait Boy was coming too?

TANYA: I did, sweetie.

KRISTA [*displaying a minor tearful explosion*]: Why do you all treat me like a child?

TANYA: Hey hey, come here.

[*Does* KRISTA *sit on* TANYA's *lap?*]

It's gonna be a real nice funeral. We'll all be there, like family.

KRISTA: He's not family!

TANYA: Hey, hey. He was a part of this place. We all went to hell and back together how many times? And Miss Ruby was there through it all. Now she's moving on and we gotta celebrate! Lord knows there's a deluxe dressing room waiting for her somewhere up there, with chilled champagne and one of those silky robes and every single lightbulb around the mirror over her dressing table is working, / casting a soft light . . .

KRISTA [half laughing]: She was always bitching about those bulbs . . .

TANYA: It was a beautiful club. Everyone was welcome.

KRISTA: I first saw Miss Ruby dance when I was sixteen. Climbed out my bedroom window and drove from Mobile to the French Quarter with my friends. And we snuck into her club and there she was, standing on her hands in the middle of a giant champagne glass, then arching her back and reaching her toes back first to her head, then to her hands, and then standing back up, then taking a bottle of champagne and somehow pouring it onto her shoulder—here—so it rolled straight down her arm off her fingers and into the mouth of some guy . . .

TANYA [quietly, kind of in her own world]: Who's going to remember us?

KRISTA: What?

TANYA: Nothing. Nothing, forget it.

[Beat. KRISTA sniffs under one of her arms.]

KRISTA: I stink.

TANYA: Go take a shower, sugar. Go on. It'll make you feel fresh and clean.

KRISTA [looking at the floor]: I don't have my room this week.

TANYA: Then go on up to my room. I've got some kiwi body wash, it'll make everything nice again.

[As KRISTA *goes up the stairs,* SHADY CHARACTER THREE *comes out of the Problem Room. At about the same time,* SISSY NA NA's *door opens, and she pokes her head out.*]

SISSY NA NA: Tanya, we taking the bus?

TANYA: No, I got a friend picking us up.

SISSY NA NA: Thank you, Jesus . . .

[SISSY NA NA *closes the door.* KRISTA *goes into* TANYA's *room.* SHADY CHARACTER THREE *kind of creeps up behind* TANYA.]

SHADY CHARACTER THREE [*meaning, "Hey Baby"*]: Hey, Bay.

TANYA: Oh God!

SHADY CHARACTER THREE: You got everything you need?

TANYA: Thank you, I do.

SHADY CHARACTER THREE: You sure?

TANYA: Definitely.

SHADY CHARACTER THREE: Aight.

[SHADY CHARACTER THREE *slinks back into the Problem Room and closes the door.* TANYA *sighs, relieved. She reaches into the pocket of her dress, pulls out a lipstick. She opens it, puts some lipstick on, returns it to her pocket. Okay, now she's ready.*]

TANYA: Well, okay!

[TANYA *claps her hands.*]

SCENE 2

[*It is several hours later.* TERRY *and* KRISTA *are in the exact same spots they were in at the top of the play. Except now,* KRISTA *has her hair pulled back, fresh from her shower,* TERRY *is maybe wearing a workday shirt, and they are both smoking. Next to the car is a garbage can with a keg in it—iced down and all.*

A car is heard driving by with Dr. John's "Right Place, Wrong Time" playing super loud. It is a crowd of tourists or maybe locals going to Jazz Fest. The car (offstage) stops at a light. KRISTA *kind of laughs and shakes her head, then she puts her cigarette in her mouth and walks toward the front of the stage. Laughing, she yells to the car.*]

KRISTA: Yeah, you think? You think?

[*She quickly lifts up her shirt, flashing her bare breasts to the car. Immediately she is hit with bunches of beads. She catches most of them.* TERRY *kind of half laughs as the car drives away, and* KRISTA *kind of nods "thank you" to the car.*]

TERRY: It ain't even Mardi Gras.

KRISTA: Whatever. Tourists think it's Mardi Gras all year round.

TERRY: You shouldn't be flashing those to just anybody.

KRISTA: Whatever.

[*She fools with the beads around her neck.*]

You ever been to Jazz Fest, Terry?

TERRY: I delivered some Porta-Potties there once. About a week before it started. I had twenty-five of 'em, all tied up with bungee cords on the back of a flatbed truck. Security waved me through, and I saw my cousin putting out a long line of trash barrels. I holla, "Hey, Boosie, look here! I got me truck full of Porta-Potties so the good people at Jazz Fest got a place to take a shit!"

[KRISTA *laughs.*]

And he laughs, and I stop the truck—this was the year after the storm, and, man, *nobody* was back yet—it was so good to see him . . . And we catch up on things, you know, Katrina talk—this cousin's in Houston, that cousin's in Salt Lake—and when I turn around to leave? My truck was gone! Just gone. And the security guard say, "That was your truck?" And I say *yes* that was my truck, and he say, "Nigga, you need a permit to park there!" And I say, "Nigga, ain't you see it full of twenty-five *Porta-Potties* for the *Jazz and Heritage Festival?*"

[KRISTA *kind of cracks up.*]

Ran around all day, on foot, trying to get that truck out of hock. I *still* got a warrant out on my ass for that truck—they say I stole it.

KRISTA: You didn't tell the company what happened?

TERRY: Shew. [*Seeing* KRISTA *smiling*] What.

KRISTA: Can you build me a house, Terry?

TERRY: You asking me to?

[*Does* KRISTA *move away? Or look down at her feet?*]

KRISTA: No, I'm not asking.

[WAYNE *enters, sorting through mail.*]

WAYNE: Where's Tanya?

KRISTA: At the store.

TERRY: At the store with Sissy Na Na.

WAYNE: She got a letter.

TERRY: Mr. Wayne, did you notice?

[WAYNE *looks up at the gutter.*]

WAYNE: Heeeeyyy. Nice job, Terry.

TERRY: I bought extra long nails and nine-gauge wire so it would
    stay real good, and I patched up the holes with some really good
    plumbers tape and spackle. I mean, you could have gotten a whole
    new gutter, but that would have been, like, five to six hundred
    dollars.

WAYNE: Aw, no, no.

TERRY: It's up there good. Not even Hurricane Katrina could pull
    down that gutter pipe.

WAYNE: Thank you, Terry.

TERRY: Here's the receipts. Now, I got the expensive nails. So it would
    hold.

WAYNE: That's okay. Sure, sure. Let me get your money together for you.

TERRY: Thank you, I appreciate it.

[WAYNE *goes into the office.*]

KRISTA: So you've never been to Jazz Fest, Terry?

TERRY: I have never been to Jazz Fest.

KRISTA: Yeah, me neither . . .

[TANYA *and* SISSY NA NA *are heard from offstage.*]

TANYA: Thank you, sweetie, no we got it, we got it.

SISSY NA NA: Bye now.

[TANYA *yelps like her ass has been pinched and she is cracking up when she comes onstage, talking to the man who just dropped them off.*]

TANYA: Yeah, those were good times, sugar, but dey ain't dere no more! I can't help that you married a debutante! You coulda had this for breakfast, lunch, and dinner!

[*The car that dropped them off is heard driving away.* TANYA *and* SISSY NA NA *carry big bags of groceries.*]

SISSY NA NA: He a customer?

TANYA: No, an old boyfriend. Believe it or not, I went to Catholic school.

TERRY: Hey, Miss Tanya.

SISSY NA NA: He smells funny.

TANYA: I know, right?

TERRY: Miss Tanya.

TANYA: Terry, there's two more bags out there on the curb—could you grab them, honey?

TERRY: Sure.

SISSY NA NA: Like antiseptic. Like he's trying to cover up his man smell.

TANYA: He lives a very careful life.

KRISTA: Did you get Cheetos?

TANYA: I did, but they're for the party.

KRISTA: Oh.

TANYA [*sounding singsongy and excited*]: We got a lot of good stuuuuu-uuuuff. Some nice ham and turkey and some Swiss cheese and we even stopped by Binder's for some fresh French bread. And Sissy's got a disco ball, / and some streamers from the Bourbon Cowboy, and I took apart one of Miss Ruby's old costumes . . .

SISSY NA NA: I got a disco ball from the Cowboy and they gave me the leftover decorations from this gay wedding reception they had, these shiny streamers that are maybe just a little bit beer soaked—ha, I hope its beer—but they'll be fabulous.

TANYA: Terry, did you get the keg?

TERRY: Look here, Miss Tanya.

TANYA: Look at that, all iced and ready to go.

TERRY: Yep.

TANYA: Thank you, sugar, I knew I could count on you.

[TANYA *gives* TERRY *a kiss on the cheek, and goes back to organize groceries. A* NURSE'S AIDE *comes out of* MISS RUBY's *room.*]

SISSY NA NA: Miss Ruby doing okay?

NURSE'S AIDE: Oh, um, yes, she's resting. There's still a lot of fluid in her lungs, it's important that she stay with her head up and her feet up. And she's . . . you're giving her Gatorade?

SISSY NA NA: Ensure.

NURSE'S AIDE: Gatorade or Ensure, as much as she can keep down. Are you . . . her . . .

KRISTA: Friends. We're like family.

NURSE'S AIDE: Oh.

KRISTA: What?

NURSE'S AIDE: Nothing.

TERRY: We're having a funeral for her today.

NURSE'S AIDE: What?

KRISTA: No, no . . .

TERRY: We are!

NURSE'S AIDE: She's, you all know she's alive in there, right? She is very much alive and in need of constant care.

SISSY NA NA: We know that, thank you.

NURSE'S AIDE: All right, well, you have the hospice number?

KRISTA: It's taped to the door.

NURSE'S AIDE [*acting kind of resigned and judgmental*]: All right.

[*The* NURSE'S AIDE *leaves.* WAYNE *comes out of the office, hands* TANYA *her letter.*]

WAYNE: Here you go, Tanya.

TANYA: Thanks.

[TANYA *takes the letter.* KRISTA *is in the process of sneaking the bag of Cheetos out of the grocery bag.*]

SISSY NA NA: When's Bait Boy coming, anyway?

TANYA: He's coming for the funeral.

WAYNE: Bait Boy's *coming*?

KRISTA: He's coming for the funeral.

WAYNE: He owes me a hundred and fifty dollars for the minifridge he threw off the balcony That Famous Night.

KRISTA: That was like four years ago.

WAYNE: Oh right, make that two hundred dollars with interest.

TERRY: Why they call him Bait Boy, anyway?

SISSY NA NA: 'Cause he was always baitin' the crowd at Cat's Meow when he worked the karaoke stage.

TANYA: 'Cause he was always baiting people, like picking / a fight.

WAYNE: No, no, he grew up fishing down in Lafouche, and his daddy made him gather the bait.

KRISTA: 'Cause he was always picking up jailbait, he likes 'em young.

SISSY NA NA: Funny he wound up with a cougar, then.

TERRY [*under his breath*]: Bait Boy.

[TANYA *opens her letter and looks at it, crossing to another part of the stage, but still listening to the group.*]

WAYNE: Hey Terry, come see.

[WAYNE *counts cash for* TERRY.]

So here's your hundred dollars, but I just wanted to check, you said you bought nails, but these are screws—on this receipt . . .

TERRY: Oh yeah, screws, I meant screws. Screws are what you need.

[KRISTA *is eating Cheetos, but nobody notices.*]

KRISTA: I'm not gonna talk to him. I'm just going to stay on the other side of the lot and give him the evil eye.

TANYA [*while reading the letter*]: That's fine, sugar, if that's what makes you feel strong . . .

SISSY NA NA: Or you can talk *a lot*, like it's no big deal that he's here.

[SISSY NA NA *says "nonchalant" with a French accent.*]

WAYNE: Did you borrow my drill?

TERRY: No, I had a friend's, I borrowed a friend's. Come see.

[WAYNE *follows* TERRY *to the gutter pipe.*]

Act nonchalant.

[KRISTA *kind of rolls her eyes and keeps eating Cheetos.*]

Look here. When Bait Boy waltzes up in here all suburban and shit, *you* gonna start casually tossing off details about your new life.

KRISTA: New life?

SISSY NA NA: Bait Boy is here for the afternoon. You can be whoever you want.

[*Maybe* SISSY NA NA *gets out some bags of decorations, or organizes some grocery bags for a second.*]

WAYNE: I just need it done right. The owners have been coming around. Too much. You feel me?

TERRY: Mm-hmm.

WAYNE: They got their eye on this place.

[TERRY *puts a hand on* WAYNE's *shoulder, or maybe both hands on both shoulders.*]

TERRY: Hey. Mr. Wayne. I gotcha.

WAYNE: Okay . . .

[*Perhaps* TERRY *goes back upstairs to his spot on the balcony and* WAYNE *settles into a chair outside his office.*]

KRISTA: Like, like maybe I can tell him that I work at a law firm.

SISSY NA NA: There you go.

KRISTA: Like maybe a paralegal? A paralegal assistant, that sounds more realistic.

SISSY NA NA: There you go—and what do you do with your free time?

KRISTA: I don't know! I don't know what to say!

SISSY NA NA: Yes you do, *yes you do*—all those men at the strip club, what do their wives do at home?

[SISSY NA NA *opens up her big handbag and starts putting makeup on* KRISTA.]

KRISTA: Um . . . go to Zumba classes and make crafty candles?

SISSY NA NA: Yes!

KRISTA: But he knows that's not me!

SISSY NA NA: You haven't seen him in three years! Now where you gonna say you living?

KRISTA: Oh God . . .

SISSY NA NA: In a condo in the warehouse district.

KRISTA: He'll never believe that.

SISSY NA NA: All right then, with your sister—you are living with your sister on the Westbank and you take the express bus over the bridge to downtown.

[TANYA *folds the letter and rejoins the group during* KRISTA's *next line.*]

KRISTA: And I'm not dating anyone, but there is this guy in the copy room who keeps flirting with me.

TANYA: Copy room! You can do better than the copy room!

WAYNE: Everything okay, Tanya?

[TANYA *makes a gesture like, "fine, fine," and starts absentmindedly eating Cheetos.*]

KRISTA: Weelll . . . then should I say—a lawyer?

SISSY NA NA: Absolutely, a *fine* lawyer.

TANYA: You deserve a lawyer.

SISSY NA NA: He keeps asking you out, but you keep saying no, because you've got a lot of work to do on your candles.

KRISTA: For a big craft fair I have coming up.

SISSY NA NA: Now *that's* a story.

TANYA: You know, it's not that hard to make those crafty candles, you just gotta get a ride out to Michaels and get ribbon and some of those little rhinestones, and I mean you can turn a five-dollar candle into a fifteen-dollar candle like *that*.

SISSY NA NA: Yeah, but does anyone really want to spend their time making butt-ugly candles?

TANYA: Well, you gotta spend your time doing something . . .

KRISTA: I thought you said Bait Boy would be impressed, that making candles would be a good thing.

SISSY NA NA: It is—it's not—I mean it *is* to a lot of people. And it *sounds* good. It's one of those things that sounds better than it actually looks.

TERRY [*from the balcony*]: My ex-wife made wineglasses.

WAYNE: She, like, blew glass?

SISSY NA NA [*suddenly sounding almost like a frat boy*]: "Blew glass," heh, heh.

TERRY [*ignoring or not hearing* SISSY NA NA]: She painted, she painted wineglasses, you know, colorful phrases, "Girls Nite Out," "Party Time," that sort of thing.

KRISTA: I can't do this.

SISSY NA NA: You look beautiful.

KRISTA [*trying out some lines*]: "And I speed walk around the lagoon at City Park every Saturday."

TANYA: With your sister.

KRISTA: With my sister.

TANYA: So you don't sound lonely.

[KRISTA *eats a Cheeto during a moment of silence, making a big crunch. Finally,* TANYA *notices* KRISTA *is eating the Cheetos.*]

Krista! Those are for the party!

KRISTA: I know, I couldn't help it. I'm nervous.

TANYA: And you've got me eating them, too! Goddamn it!

WAYNE: It's okay, baby, we can get more.

TANYA: The party is in three hours.

SISSY NA NA:	KRISTA:
We can get Cheetos anywhere.	I'm sorry.

TANYA: I know, I *know*, that's *not* the point. (God.)

[TANYA *is trying in vain to wipe the orange Cheeto dust off her hands.*]

SISSY NA NA:	WAYNE:
Baby, what's the matter?	Geez.

KRISTA [*looking in the bag of Cheetos*]: There's still a lot left.

TANYA: Nothing, it's just—one of my . . . one of my kids is trying to find me.

KRISTA: One of your kids?

TANYA: One of the kids I gave up. When things were really bad. She's turning twenty. And she's trying to find her birth mom.

| SISSY NA NA: | TERRY: | WAYNE: |
| Oh baby. | That's deep. | What are you going to do? |

TANYA: I don't know what I'm going to do. What should I do?

KRISTA: Well, do you want to see her?

WAYNE: Maybe you should see her. On neutral territory.

TANYA: What, like in a restaurant or something?

WAYNE: Yeah, like in a restaurant.

SISSY NA NA: My cousin met his birth mom, and it really fucked him up. Because his birth mom had, like, totally gotten her act together—she was, like, a lawyer in a million-dollar house, and his *adoptive parents*, who raised him, were, like, a mess—they got divorced when he was four, and his adoptive mom is on disability and addicted to pain pills and his adoptive dad went to prison for two years for robbing a Laundromat.

WAYNE: How do you rob a Laundromat?

SISSY NA NA: You jimmy the change machine.

[*Right before* KRISTA *says the word "hooker" below,* WAYNE *intentionally gets up and heads inside.*]

KRISTA: Yeah, so you should find out, Tanya, find out if your kid's adoptive parents are, like, *rich*, because if they are, then when your daughter finds out her birth mom is a hooker, she'll feel, you know, like she got a good deal.

[KRISTA *meant well, but that comment did not land so great.*]

　. . . What?

SISSY NA NA: Krista.

KRISTA: No, I mean she'll think you sacrificed to give her a better life, a richer life.

SISSY NA NA: Krista—

[*Is there a moment where everyone looks at* TANYA? TANYA *takes a breath, then she looks at the grocery bags.*]

TANYA: Sandwiches, I've got to start the sandwiches.

[TANYA *starts taking bags of luncheon meat and bread out of the grocery bags as though readying herself to make the sandwiches?*]

WAYNE: Hey Krista, can I see you?

KRISTA: I don't know, can you?

WAYNE: Just come here.

KRISTA: What?

WAYNE: Just come here.

[KRISTA *walks over.*]

SISSY NA NA: All right, we gotta get this party started . . .

[SISSY NA NA *heads up to her room to fetch party decorations.*]

WAYNE: Listen, Krista, you cannot use the *h* word around me.

KRISTA: What?

WAYNE: When you are talking about Tanya.

KRISTA: The *h* word . . .

SISSY NA NA: How many ducks did you get?

KRISTA [*to* WAYNE]:   TANYA:
   Hot?   A lot.

WAYNE: No, no Krista, when you are talking about Tanya's profession, you cannot use the *h* word around me because I cannot know what Tanya does when her "friends" come to visit.

KRISTA: Ohh. Okay, all right. But I mean, really, Wayne, you know what is going on.

WAYNE: Krista, look, who knows who is watching us right now, I mean you could be wearing a wire—

[KRISTA *flashes her tits, laughing.*]

KRISTA: I'm not wearing no wire. You watch too much TV.

WAYNE: Krista!

KRISTA: Those crime shows, serial killers duct-taping women into crawl spaces and shit—

WAYNE: *Krista!* . . . Look, I'm under a lot of pressure from the owners to fill these rooms and make some money, 'cause if we don't make some money—

KRISTA: Nobody cares about us.

WAYNE: Just don't use the *h* word, okay? It's not . . . she's better than that, okay? She's better.

[KRISTA *kind of shrugs and backs away as* SISSY NA NA *comes out of her room with a disco ball.*]

SISSY NA NA: Now, look here, we have a funeral to throw and we are going to throw it in style. Terry, go ask Mr. Wayne for that old card table and some duct tape and put it up here, but be sure you tape the fakakta leg good, now—Tanya, unpack the meat and I'll bring it up to my minifridge.

[TERRY *heads in to get the table.*]

TANYA: I was gonna make them now.

SISSY NA NA: No, we'll do it later, when there's more help. We are going to *transform* this place into the most beautiful living funeral you have ever seen. We'll hang the disco ball there, and when night falls, we'll spin it and hit it with flashlights, and we will swag the streamers so they run from here all the way to there, and Miss Ruby will feel like she is young again, back in her club, in her glory days. Everybody is going to feel beautiful at this party, you hear me? *Everyone is going to feel beautiful.* Everyone is going to realize that each one of us is in charge of

[*While* SISSY NA NA *speaks, she finds a glass jar of glitter. She sprinkles glitter on people either when she says "transform" or "Miss Ruby will feel like she is young again."*]

KRISTA [*quoting "Gold Digger"*]: Get down girl, go head, get down, get down girl, go head—

WAYNE [*laughing*]: Shake it, girl.

holding up a very special part
of the universe, and without
each one of us, the universe
would just come crashing
down—and oh, look at this, if
it isn't Bait Boy.

[BAIT BOY *has entered, with his stepdaughter,* ZOE. *They look totally at odds with the environment of the Hummingbird.* BAIT BOY *wears pressed khakis and a patterned, button-down short-sleeved shirt and shoes that veer toward dress shoes. Whatever outfit* ZOE *wears looks like it just came off a mannequin at the Gap: a complete outfit.* BAIT BOY *holds a platter of fancy-looking sandwiches.* ZOE *carries a bag that could hold a computer. When they see him,* TANYA *has her hands full of bags of luncheon meat,* KRISTA'S *head is in her hoodie, and* TERRY *is looking at the leg of the table.*]

BAIT BOY: Hey, everybody.

[*There is a moment, like, all right, are these people happy to see this guy or not? And then everyone launches into hellos, almost like all is forgiven, very animated and polite.* KRISTA *hangs back, half watching, half in her own head.*]

[*These next four speeches should be performed simultaneously. The second half of* WAYNE'S *joke should be clearly heard. When* TANYA *asks* ZOE *her name,* ZOE *replies. While everyone else greets* BAIT BOY, KRISTA *moves away, up the stairs, watching them.*]

WAYNE: Bait Boy, it's good to see you, look at you, you clean up real good. I could mistake you for a frikken Adams and Reese lawyer—a peach-colored shirt? Really? What has Atlanta done to our boy? Hey Bait Boy, here's a good one for you: what's the difference between your mother and a washing machine? When I drop a load in my washing machine, it doesn't beg me for more.

[*Realizing* ZOE's *presence*] Oh sorry, sorry, how old are you? Sorry.

TANYA: Hi there, you sweet little fresh-faced boy, oh my god you look eighteen, and your eyes are so clear! And this is? . . . Zoe, well what an exotic name, sorry my hands are full of meat, here give me a hug, no, go on just reach around and give me a hug, there you go. Miss Ruby's been asking for you, you know. I know that's why Sissy called you, that's why Sissy called you.

TERRY: Hey there Bait Boy, looking good, looking good. I remember that time when we fixed up the stage at the Tropical Isle, we worked together, we got paid good for that job. Good to see you, good to see you. You happy to see me? Sure you're happy to see me. Bet you didn't think I'd still be around . . .

SISSY NA NA: Bait Boy I like to slap you upside your head! Never call! Never write! Probably living in some mansion up in Hotlanta, some "Real Housewives" shit I bet, come here, I like to bend you over my knee and whip you, come here, I'm gonna whip you, come here I'm gonna—yeah you like that don't you—Bait Boy, how do you always come out on top—hello Zoe, you can call me Sissy Na Na. Shit, no, come on, you know I love you, really.

[*When these four speeches end,* BAIT BOY *speaks. Maybe* ZOE *stands in front of him, his hand on her shoulder?*]

BAIT BOY [*calling to* KRISTA, *up on the stairs*]: Hi Krista.

KRISTA: Hey.

TANYA: Doesn't Krista look beautiful, Bait Boy?

KRISTA: Tanya!

BAIT BOY: Actually, I wanted to mention, this may sound weird but I go by Greg now.

[*Beat.*]

SISSY NA NA: Greg?

BAIT BOY: Yes, Greg. For, like, three years now—Greg.

WAYNE: That's your given name?

BAIT BOY: Gregory actually, but Greg is fine.

TERRY [*trying it out*]: Greg.

SISSY NA NA [*maybe talking like a fake businessman*]: Greg.

[SISSY NA NA *and a couple folks laugh.*]

BAIT BOY: That's right.

TANYA [*referring to the platter of sandwiches*]: Whatcha got there, Greg?

[SISSY NA NA *kind of snickers.*]

BAIT BOY: Oh it's a platter of finger sandwiches, I picked them up from Whole Foods. They're really nice, the ham sandwiches have truffle oil on them, actually.

SISSY NA NA: "Actually."

KRISTA: Tanya bought luncheon meat and French bread. We were going to make our own sandwiches.

BAIT BOY: Oh well, put that stuff in the fridge, you can have it later, really, there's plenty.

KRISTA: Tanya makes good sandwiches.

TANYA: No, he's right, I'll put this stuff away. I mean, his are already made. We can make a lunch with these, or a late-night snack.

[TANYA *packs the meat back in the bags.* SISSY NA NA *and* KRISTA *watch from the stairs or maybe the balcony.* SISSY NA NA *maybe hugs* KRISTA *from behind, very intimate, like a sister but also like a boyfriend.* ZOE *wanders around the parking lot, taking pictures with her cell phone.*]

BAIT BOY: Hey, Wayne! The place looks really great.

WAYNE: Yeah, Terry just did some work on it. He fixed the . . . so what are you up to these days, Bait Boy—

BAIT BOY: Greg.

WAYNE [*continuing*]: I hear you got a real job?

SISSY NA NA: He looks pale. Waxy.

KRISTA: No he doesn't.

BAIT BOY: The rumors are true! I sell advertising for Joyce's trade magazines.

WAYNE: Joyce, that's her name?

BAIT BOY: Yeah, she owns a whole group of / them—

[SISSY NA NA *and* KRISTA *listen to* BAIT BOY *and* WAYNE.]

WAYNE: Right, she's a / businesswoman.

BAIT BOY: One for professional fishermen,

WAYNE: Oh that sounds—

BAIT BOY: One for the train / industry,

WAYNE: Oh that / sounds

BAIT BOY: And I make calls to
   businesses—

WAYNE: Reeeeeeal / interesting.

BAIT BOY: That might be interested in advertising, advertising in the magazine.

   It's great. I work from home.

WAYNE: So what's it like, eh?
   Having a sugar mama?

BAIT BOY: It's not like that, /
   Wayne. Wayne.

WAYNE: And I mean, is she, like,
   a hot sugar mama? Like, ach-
   ing for young shlong when
   you come home after a long
   hard day? 'Cause you always
   liked 'em young. Young looking, I mean.

[BAIT BOY's *cell phone rings, he
checks it.*]

   I'm just saying.

BAIT BOY: I gotta take this.

[*To* ZOE]

   It's your momma.

[BAIT BOY *crosses to the office to
take the phone call.*]

SISSY NA NA: Like he's all blocked
   up. Like a nasty ole sink.

[SISSY NA NA *pulls* KRISTA *into
her room.*]

[ZOE *has wandered near* TERRY,
who is still fixing the table.]

ZOE [*to* TERRY]: She's a little
   nervous.

TERRY: Who dat?

ZOE: My mom. She couldn't come, she's got a conference.

TERRY: Mm-hmm.

ZOE: I'm here to make sure he comes back home.

[ZOE *stays near* TERRY, *gazing around the space.* TANYA *is heading upstairs with bags of luncheon meat.*]

WAYNE: Hey Tanya, I can put that in the fridge in the office.

TANYA: Oh, okay, thanks.

[*She hands it to him and keeps going.* ZOE *turns back to* TERRY.]

ZOE: So do you live here?

TERRY: No baby, I'm the handyman.

[ZOE *watches* TERRY *fix the table.*]

WAYNE [*to* TANYA *as she goes up the stairs*]: Hey, where are you going?

TANYA: Up to my room to put on some lipstick.

WAYNE: Your lipstick is in the pocket of your dress.

TANYA: No it's not.

WAYNE: You have kept lipstick in the pocket of your dress since you were sixteen.

TANYA: I just need one.

WAYNE: You don't need one. You've got us.

TANYA: It's just so stressful . . .

WAYNE: You are an extraordinary woman, Tanya. You have taken a very unusual path through life and you have held your head up high—

TANYA: Gimme a break, Wayne. I've been a terrible mother, a terrible grocery store cashier, a terrible part-time student, a terrible waitress, and a terrible citizen of the United States because I don't pay a dime in taxes.

WAYNE: Look at this beautiful party you organized—

TANYA: I just need one—

WAYNE: Tanya, stay with us. Stay.

[TANYA *relents and heads back down, toward the bags of food and decorations, as* KRISTA *and* SISSY NA NA *emerge from* SISSY NA NA's *room.*]

TANYA: All right.

WAYNE: Thank you, baby.

TANYA [*not wanting to hear it*]: La la la la la la . . .

KRISTA: So what's your wife's name, Bait Boy?

BAIT BOY: Joyce.

[SISSY NA NA *can barely suppress her giggle.*]

What?

[KRISTA *and* SISSY NA NA *laugh together.*]

SISSY NA NA: Nothing, nothing. It's a fine name.

KRISTA: Greg and Joyce.

TANYA [*forceful, to herself*]: All right! We gotta get these decorations going!

SISSY NA NA: And Zoe, how did you get the name Zoe?

ZOE: My mom spent a lot of time in Greece when she was a kid and there are a lot of Zoes in Greece.

SISSY NA NA: I was in *Grease* when I was in high school. I played Kenickie, actually.

ZOE: Oh no, I meant Greece the country, the country named Greece.

SISSY NA NA: I know.

ZOE: What?

BAIT BOY: Zoe was hoping to talk to all of you, / actually, she has a project at school, for sociology, where she has to interview—okay, okay.

ZOE: I got it, Greg. Greg, I can explain it, let me explain it. It's for my sociology class. I'm supposed to interview at least three people from the same subculture.

SISSY NA NA: Subculture?

ZOE: Right.

SISSY NA NA: Meaning, you live in a "culture," and you are coming *down* to us?

ZOE [*in a clear, direct, overconfident manner*]: No, I'm not assuming that.

SISSY NA NA: Hm.

ZOE: Greg has told me some amazing stories about the community here at the Hummingbird Hotel.

BAIT BOY: Just about how we were like family, how we looked out for each other because most of us had no family.

SISSY NA NA: You talk about us like we're gone.

BAIT BOY: No, it's me. I'm gone.

TANYA: Krista, figure out how to put these paper ducks together, here—

[TANYA *hands a box of flat paper ducks to* KRISTA *as* ZOE *continues.*]

ZOE: Greg showed me the article about Miss Ruby—

BAIT BOY: The one in the *Gambit.*

SISSY NA NA: They spelled my name wrong.

ZOE: And he talked about her as
a kind of mother figure, and
it got me thinking about . . .
about tribes.

TANYA: Plates, cooler, music, napkins . . .

SISSY NA NA: Like tribes in
Africa? Like, we supposed
to have bones through our
noses?

ZOE: No, I mean—

BAIT BOY: It's just a school assignment. She just needs to interview you.

ZOE: I won't name names.

SISSY NA NA: Or if you do, at least spell them right.

BAIT BOY: Hey Sissy, what's your real name again?

SISSY NA NA: My real name is Sissy Na Na.

BAIT BOY: You know what I mean.

SISSY NA NA: You know what I mean. Don't get it twisted.

TANYA: Bait Boy, come help me with these streamers.

BAIT BOY [*to* TANYA]: Sure.

[BAIT BOY *crosses to* TANYA *to help her.* SISSY NA NA'*s phone alarm goes off; she pulls her phone out of her pocket.*]

SISSY NA NA: I gotta go give Miss Ruby her meds.

ZOE: See—that, I just want to write about that.

SISSY NA NA: About what? I'm going upstairs to give a dying lady her Oxycontin because she was so confused last night she pulled the morphine drip out her arm.

ZOE: See, you've created a family, and, I'm guessing, a hierarchy inside the family—

BAIT BOY: Zoe—

ZOE: And a shared language, rituals, responsibilities, so that you can survive—

SISSY NA NA: Oh, help me Rhonda—	TANYA [*standing in front of the broken down car*]: Terry baby, can you turn this car into a bar?
[SISSY NA NA *is heading up to* MISS RUBY'*s room.*]	
	TERRY: All right—
BAIT BOY: Come on Sissy, just talk to her.	TANYA [*under her breath*]: Just use whatever you can find . . .
SISSY NA NA: I gotta get this done.	[TERRY *goes in search of wood.*]

BAIT BOY [*referring to the interview*]: Hey Sissy, help your boy out.

SISSY NA NA: My what?

BAIT BOY [*smiling, like old times*]: Your boy. Help him out.

SISSY NA NA: All right, Bait Boy, but only if I can call you Bait Boy and only if you do an Irish Car Bomb with me—

BAIT BOY: Oh God—

SISSY NA NA: Like old times.

BAIT BOY: Here we go—

SISSY NA NA: To preserve the ritual of our subculture.

[ZOE *looks at* BAIT BOY *like, yes, yes, please?*]

BAIT BOY: All right, all right.

SISSY NA NA: There ya go, Bait Boy. Hook, line, and sinker.

[SISSY NA NA *goes into* MISS RUBY'S *room.*]

BAIT BOY: So how is this going to work? Is Miss Ruby going to come down?

TANYA: We're going to bring her out a little later, just for a little while. She gets really tired, everything overwhelms her, so we'll let people go in two at a time to say hello, and then she'll make an appearance at the end of the party.

BAIT BOY: Can she walk?

TANYA: Ha!

[TERRY *returns with wood to start turning the car into a bar.*]

TERRY: So what's your deal, Bait Boy, you all set up there in Atlanta?

BAIT BOY: Looks that way. I mean I have a job, and a, well, a-a partner. It's a nice place to live.

ZOE: I *hate* Atlanta. I can't wait to get out.

BAIT BOY: This one's only applying to colleges that are at least a day's drive away.

ZOE: Chicago, Northampton, Boston—

TERRY: Why you hate it?

ZOE: Ohio, New Haven—but that's a long shot. Because Atlanta is, like, *blech*, cookie-cutter corporate land, there's nothing authentic there, it's like business-casual men in sky-blue polo shirts and "community placemaking" and women with fresh highlights and Brazilian blowouts.

TERRY: I could show you an Atlanta that is not like that.

[WAYNE *comes out of the office, and either sweeps or sits in a chair and watches all this happen. As he does, he sings under his breath.*]

WAYNE [*singing as* ZOE *continues to talk*]: Oom poo pa doo . . . *You know they call me the most . . .*

ZOE: Oh, well, sure, there are pockets of cool local culture in the city, but you have to be born into that, and I was born on another track, and if I stay there, I'm just going to atrophy—atrophize? Into this perfect little, I don't know, wife.

[ZOE *shudders.*]

TERRY: Now, I've never met a perfect wife.

ZOE: They're in Atlanta, believe me.

[*Around here,* SISSY NA NA *comes out of* MISS RUBY's *room and starts hanging the shiny beer-soaked streamers she salvaged from the Bourbon Cowboy.* BAIT BOY *approaches* KRISTA.]

BAIT BOY: So! Krista! What's going on with you? Are you still dancing at—

KRISTA: No, no I'm working as a paralegal assistant.

BAIT BOY: Oh really, where?

WAYNE [*singing as* KRISTA *and* BAIT BOY *continue to talk.*]: *I'm gonna make up all the words to this song . . . You know they call me the most . . .*

KRISTA: It's downtown. I take the bus over—over from the Westbank.

BAIT BOY: That's amazing! Are you living over there now?

KRISTA: Yeah. At my sister's. To save money.

[SISSY NA NA *gives* KRISTA *a big thumbs-up, but so* BAIT BOY *can't see her do so.*]

BAIT BOY: Awesome. I figured you were still living—

KRISTA: No, no, I don't live here anymore.

ZOE [*to* KRISTA]: Oh, you don't live here anymore?

KRISTA: No, no, I don't live here anymore.

ZOE: Interesting.

KRISTA: Really?

ZOE: No, I mean it's interesting that you come back, I mean for important events.

[ZOE *slips her iPad out of her purse.*]

BAIT BOY [*to* ZOE]: Miss Ruby is important to a lot of people.

WAYNE [*singing as* ZOE *continues to talk.*]: *And I won't stop trying till I create a disturbance in your mind* . . .

ZOE [*to* KRISTA]: OK, so, could you name three reasons why Miss Ruby is important to you?

[ZOE *presses a button on her iPad:* bing!]

KRISTA: Wait are you . . . are you recording this?

ZOE: Yes, I—

KRISTA: You can't just record people! Bait Boy, what's wrong with her? God, I mean, you're gonna make a terrible journalist, you little shit.

WAYNE [*sings, then speaks*]: Create a disturbance in your—

[*Responding to* TANYA:] Sure, why not?

ZOE [*responding to* BAIT BOY]: Oh shit, right, shit, she—I knew that, *fuck*, why do I fuck *everything* up!

WAYNE [*to* ZOE]: Hey, hey, sweetie, go easy—life's too short. Now get Uncle Wayne a beer and let's have a chat. Don't worry, Bait Boy, I got this—Terry, the keg is cold, right?

BAIT BOY: Zoe, turn it off, come on, baby, you gotta ask—

TANYA: Krista—

Zoe, go chat up Wayne. Wayne, will you talk to this nice young lady?

BAIT BOY [*going close to* ZOE]: You gotta ask, okay sweetie? Ask before you press Record, and then get their approval on tape—

TERRY: Cold as my ex-wife.

[WAYNE *and* TERRY *laugh.* ZOE *goes to the keg and gets* WAYNE *a beer.*]

BAIT BOY [*resuming his conversation with* KRISTA]: So how's the whole crazy gang? Is Wolf still working the door at Goldmine?

KRISTA: Yeah, he's still there, but just on weekends now. He actually bought a house—

BAIT BOY: Wolf? A house?

KRISTA: Well, like, half a house or something, with his cousin. It needs a lot of work.

BAIT BOY: That's crazy—

KRISTA [*blurting out a lie, a little clumsily*]: I have a savings account.

BAIT BOY [*being sly and flirty? showing amazement that they are living the straight life?*]: Well. That must mean you have a checking account.

KRISTA [*smiling, less clumsily*]: They're linked.

BAIT BOY: Remember how we used to count our quarters?

KRISTA: And nickels. And pennies. And bring them to the grocery store . . .

BAIT BOY: And dump them all into that old change-counting machine . . .

[KRISTA *smiles.* BAIT BOY *pulls* KRISTA *aside, or speaks this next part super low.*]

Hey, I didn't tell Zoe about us.

KRISTA: Oh . . .

BAIT BOY: I mean, she's just a kid. And you know it's like, I come back here, I look around, and I'm like, did I really live here? Did all those things really happen?

KRISTA [*in a singsongy manner?*]: They happened.

TANYA [*throwing* BAIT BOY *a roll of streamers from the balcony*]: Hey, catch—

[BAIT BOY *catches the streamers.* TANYA *throws him another roll.*]

And this is the accent color.

BAIT BOY [*to* TANYA]: You want both?

TANYA: Just alternate them, or twist them or something. Oh look how nice it is already looking.

BAIT BOY: See Krista? Everything turned out just great, for both of us.

[BAIT BOY *gives her a quick, casual kiss on the cheek.* KRISTA's *face falls.* ZOE *brings the beer to* WAYNE.]

WAYNE: Thank you, sweetie. Now what is this, a school project?

ZOE: It's an honors paper, about subcultures.

WAYNE: Well, we are definitely *sub*culture around here. What's lower than the gutter?

ZOE: I don't know, what?

WAYNE: Us fools, that's what.

[TANYA *and* SISSY NA NA *laugh.*]

So what do you wanna know?

[ZOE *is getting her iPad ready.*]

ZOE: Do you mind if I record you?

WAYNE: Yes, I mind.

ZOE: Thanks, I—oh.

WAYNE: I said I mind.

ZOE: It's just for a school project, I mean it won't go out of the school.

WAYNE: *I said I mind.* Listen. With your two ears. Like they did in the old days.

[*Maybe* ZOE *puts away her iPad, digs around in her purse, finds a notepad and a pen.*]

ZOE: So, how long have you been manager of the Hummingbird?

WAYNE: Fifteen years, give or take.

ZOE: And how did you first come to the job?

WAYNE: "Come to" the job?

ZOE: Yeah.

WAYNE: Let's see . . .

[*As* WAYNE *speaks to* ZOE, *the rest of the characters decorate and listen: streamers, boas, feather fans, table decorations. Eventually* TERRY *helps* SISSY NA NA *hang the disco ball from under the balcony—he has to get a ladder to do this. It is like the Hummingbird is blooming as* WAYNE *tells this story.*]

WAYNE: So my great-grandfather was a milliner from Kilkenny—we called him Daddo—and he came to New Orleans through Liverpool and opened Murphy's Hat Shop on Common Street over on the edge of the Quarter. It was a bustling place, people lined up out the door, three to four girls sewing hats in the back room— these were women's hats, of a high quality, purples and greens, feathers and bows. I remember one he made with a stuffed French duck sewn right into the top—

TANYA: Oh wait, I have those lights!

[TANYA runs up into her room.]

Hand to God! Now, when I was little, I'd sneak into the back room to visit the girls, and they would stop sewing and dote on me: pat me on the head, scratch me behind my ears, feed me sugar cubes—almost like I was a horse! Even at seven years old I would get just a little excited down there—they'd wear their pincushions on their wrists—I'd get just a little tickle down there, and this friend of mine has been

TERRY: A real French duck? On top of a hat? Come on—a real duck?

[TANYA comes out of her room and down the stairs holding several strings of party lights.]

getting me into a whole lot of trouble ever since.

[*To* TANYA] Only 'cause you keep turning me down— Tanya and I have known each other since we were fifteen— It was an incredible shop, Murphy's Hats, and my great-grandfather was an expert milliner, so of course he wanted to pass his craft on to his son, my grandpa, we called him Pa*paw*. But my great-grandfather was a per- fectionist—he would check every tiny stitch my Pa*paw* would sew—make him undo entire hats and start over, he was *maniacal*. And so even- tually my Pa*paw* was like fuck it, you make the hats and I'll just work the cash register and wait for you to die, Old man. And that's what he did, for years— worked the cash register in the mornings and spent the rest of his day down at the race track, developing a wicked taste for the horses.

Of course I remember.

TANYA: Wayne's been a flirt since he cut his baby teeth.

Oh, well . . .

[*Handing the tangle of lights to* ZOE] Here, untangle while you talk.

[*To* WAYNE] Language.

He had his own special seat in the grandstand, remember?

WAYNE: So years pass. My great-grandfather dies. Huge funeral. My Papaw inherits the business. By this time, he's basically a gambling addict who doesn't know jack shit about hatmaking. So what do you think he does? Hang on—

[WAYNE *goes to the keg to top up his beer.*]

KRISTA: Bait Boy, that shirt.

BAIT BOY: What?

KRISTA: Nothing.

TANYA: Wayne, it's too early to be drinking like that.

WAYNE: Ah blah blah blah, it's Jazz Fest, Tanya.

TANYA: Any excuse . . .

BAIT BOY [*to* KRISTA, *again re: his shirt*]: What?

KRISTA: NUH-THING.

TANYA: It looks nice, GREG.

SISSY NA NA: It's very presentable, very spring.

KRISTA: I'm just saying.

BAIT BOY: What?

SISSY NA NA: It is the clothes of a man named Greg.

BAIT BOY: That's my name.

SISSY NA NA: And so it suits you, that's all I'm saying.

[WAYNE *has returned to* ZOE.]

WAYNE: So what does he do? He switches the whole thing over to factory hats! Hats made by *machine* that arrive on a truck from St. Louis! And, I mean you can pick your color or pattern on your hatband, but—

[*Responding to* TANYA:] Yeah, I mean, they were way nicer than the crap you find in stores these days, but there were no girls in the back anymore, just my poor grandmother, taking inventory of the boxes, check, check, check . . . bored out of her skull. And so look, after a year or two of Papaw dicking around at the front counter, yapping it up with his racetrack buddies, this time Mamaw was like, fuck it, I'm starting my own business here in the back room. And she starts making boutonnieres—you know, flowers and corsages for proms, weddings, each one its own little handmade miracle. And *boom*. Mamaw becomes a local celebrity.

TANYA: They were very nice hats—I bought my ex-husband one.

[*Under her breath, at Wayne's "fuck it":*] Wayne.

66

TERRY: Lines all the way down Common Street.

WAYNE: Yes. It becomes a New Orleans tradition, going down to Murphy's Hats to get your flowers.

TERRY: And the Uptowners, they would pay people like me to hold their place in line! I'm serious.

WAYNE:	TERRY:
He's not lying.	No lie.

WAYNE: You kids still wear corsages at your proms?

ZOE: Some kids do, but . . .

[ZOE's *face indicates that it is pretty dorky to get one.*]

WAYNE: Ah, now that's a shame.

ZOE: It's just a flower.

WAYNE: It's a ritual. Write that down . . .

ZOE: What?

WAYNE: It's a ritual . . .

KRISTA [*referring to* BAIT BOY's *shirt*]: You look like one of those guys who sit behind a desk at a bank.

WAYNE: Ya gotta have rituals . . .

[WAYNE *watches as* ZOE *writes it down.*]	BAIT BOY: Come on, I mean, what, does this make you feel better?
	[BAIT BOY *untucks his shirt.*]
	KRISTA: Yes.

[SHADY CHARACTER TWO *and* SHADY CHARACTER THREE *come out of the Problem Room.*]

BAIT BOY: And maybe this?

[*He unbuttons a button or two.*]

KRISTA: Yeeaaah, there you go.

[BAIT BOY *kind of rolls his eyes.*]

ZOE [*indicating the* SHADY CHARACTERS]: Who's that?

BAIT BOY: It's just a shirt, Krista.

WAYNE: Nobody. They just rented a room.

Sissy, it's fine. They pay on time, that's all I'm saying. Sissy, it's fine, thanks for your concern—

All right, so then my *father*, well, my father—*I got it, Sissy*—so my father, well, nobody taught him how to make hats, so after high school he starts apprenticing as an air-conditioning tech, installing and repairing air-conditioning units. And he meets my mom and marries my mom, then I was born, and then he moves the family out here to Kenner to a house on West Esplanade—which is not *nearly* as exotic as it sounds—and my

SISSY NA NA: Wayne, you creating a *situation* with that room. Looking the other way is the best way to drive off the road.

You're slipping, Wayne, this place is slipping.

sister is born, and she had a mild case of MS, like medium case of MS, and so mostly I just ran the streets, I mean, my dad never talked, he just sat in his chair and watched TV till the day he keeled over, died. But I mean, there was nothing *traumatic*, like divorces or a terrible car accident, we were just—regular. And the next thing I knew my grandma sold Murphy's Hats to pay off P*apaw*'s gambling debts. And I don't think I quite realized what was happening that day, standing outside Murphy's Hats, watching my grandmother lock the doors for the last time. It was just me and her, I'm not sure why, maybe I gave her a ride, and when she turned that key I remember sighing inside and thinking, well, I guess I'll just be an air-conditioner repair tech, like my dad. I mean that's noble enough work, right? Keeping people comfortable in their own homes . . .

[ZOE *walks over to* TANYA *with the strings of light, now untangled.* TERRY *finishes with the disco ball about at this point.*]

ZOE: Here.

TANYA: Thank you, honey.

ZOE: It's missing a light.

TANYA: Thank you.

[ZOE *goes back over to* WAYNE.]

[*A moment passes while* WAYNE *thinks about where his life went wrong.*]

ZOE: And so, how did you get this job?

[*Another moment passes.*]

WAYNE: This job? Oh baby, that's a really long story, I don't know . . .

[TANYA *notices* KRISTA *has abandoned the ducks.*]

TANYA: *Krista! You didn't finish the ducks!*

KRISTA: Oh, yeah, I didn't.

TANYA [*shaking her head*]: Krista . . .

ZOE: Why ducks?

TANYA: In the old days, Miss Ruby had a duck pond, around the edge of the stage—

SISSY NA NA: She would fill it with water, like a little river all the way around the stage. And she would put live baby ducks in there, and they would swim around—

ZOE: During the show?

SISSY NA NA: During the show, yes—

TANYA: Miss Ruby's acts always had nature in them, like she'd be dressed as a panther—

WAYNE [*to* ZOE, *clarifying*]: But a hot panther, a sexy panther—

TANYA: And she'd pretend to eat the chicks, oh it was hilarious—

BAIT BOY: Did anyone tape her lectures?

SISSY NA NA:	ZOE:
Oh lord, the lectures!	Like lectures at school?

TANYA: They were once a month on Sundays, we would all gather in the club—

TERRY: A church for the churchless—

TANYA: Lectures on sex and sexuality.

KRISTA: On life.

SISSY NA NA: And in the beginning there was—

ALL [*except* ZOE]: Sex!

[*They all kind of laugh.*]

ZOE: And no one taped them?

SISSY NA NA: No, nobody taped them, and so they are gone forever and nobody will ever know.

[KRISTA *moves to comfort* SISSY NA NA.]

TANYA: No one talks about her getting shut down, you hear? She doesn't remember, and she doesn't *need* to remember. She doesn't remember Katrina, she doesn't remember the tax man or the repo man, she doesn't remember That Terrible Morning when they literally had to drag her from the club kicking and crying, prying her fingers from the tabletops, the door handles—that woman has experienced enough pain, she does not need one more drop of pain at her own funeral.

ZOE: What kind of pain?

TANYA: What?

ZOE: What kind of pain did she experience in her life?

TANYA: A lot of it.

ZOE: Can you give me an example?

TANYA: An example isn't the whole picture.

ZOE: Well, I know, but, I mean, of course this project is from my perspective and I have to acknowledge that—

TANYA: How long are you here?

ZOE: For the afternoon.

[TANYA *and* SISSY NA NA *crack up.*]

TANYA:	SISSY NA NA:
The afternoon.	She gonna tell our story by hanging out for *the afternoon.*

ZOE: Guys. I live in Atlanta. I'm in high school.

[SISSY NA NA *gets real serious. When she says below "slit his wrists instead,"* BAIT BOY *tries to interject, "Hey . . . Sissy Na Na."*]

SISSY NA NA: When I was in high school, when I was in *junior* high, my stepdad kicked me out after he caught me wearing my sister's bra and panties. I got my clavicle broken *here* and then *here.* You wanna know how it got broke? No you don't want to know how it got broke. That was also the year my uncle, who was an alcoholic, moved in with us, so I slept on the couch while he tried to detox in my room but decided to slit his wrists instead. And he didn't die, no he didn't die, he just roamed around our house with those nasty bandages around his wrists for a month. And then my sister, the smart one—she was so fucking smart—takes a bad mix of pills at a house party and gets herself hit by a car trying to walk home and winds up in a wheelchair, and she basically knows who we are now, but that's about all she knows. All that when I'm in junior high. *Junior high.* And Katrina didn't hit till I was grown.

ZOE: All right.

[BAIT BOY *puts a hand on* ZOE's *shoulder*.]

SISSY NA NA: You can't get the whole picture. It's not yours to get.

TANYA: She's just trying to do her best, do good in school, right baby?

KRISTA: High school is hard. I don't know how anybody finishes high school.

TERRY: Don't matter no more anyhow, 'cause then, shit, you got to get into college. My daughter in Baton Rouge, she's trying. But she's a B student.

TANYA: B's are good.

ZOE: Not anymore. Not anymore they're not.

TANYA: Even I went to college for a while.

ZOE: Not today you wouldn't.

[*Everyone kind of looks at* ZOE.]

Well you wouldn't. It's a fucking shark tank.

BAIT BOY: All she's saying is, there's a world out there y'all don't know nothing about.

SISSY NA NA: Like grammar?

ZOE: Well why is this place called the Hummingbird?

SISSY NA NA [*acting almost like she'd forgotten, or hadn't thought about it for a while*]: The Hummingbird?

[ZOE *points to the sign*.]

ZOE: Are there a lot of hummingbirds in New Orleans?

WAYNE: I got a pamphlet, a pamphlet from the forties, hold on.

[WAYNE *gets up and goes into the office.*]

KRISTA: It sounds nice. A little bird breathing, pressing out into the sticks and mud and old gum wrappers it used to make its nest. Keeping itself warm, maybe keeping an egg warm . . .

TANYA: Hummingbirds eat sugar water . . . they like it dyed red.

WAYNE [*handing* ZOE *a crumbling pamphlet*]: "Luxury accommodations in the City That Care Forgot."

TANYA: Ha! What happened to the luxury?

ZOE: Wait, is there a pool? With a swim-up bar?

BAIT BOY: Oh no, that got covered up way before I lived here.

WAYNE: A girl—

TANYA: Wayne.

WAYNE: —drowned.

[WAYNE *is like, "What?"* TANYA *is like, "Let's not talk about that."*]

ZOE [*looking at the hotel*]: This whole thing used to be painted bright pink.

[*Does everybody look around for half a second, meaning for a moment they see their lot in life?*]

[SISSY NA NA *digs through the bags, taking out brightly colored dollar-store tablecloths. She sings and shakes her booty as she works.* TERRY *joins in too, maybe spinning* SISSY NA NA *at some point.* SISSY NA NA *sings the words to the song intentionally wrong: "No it ain't my fault . . . You claim her / I'll bang her / It ain't my fault."*]

BAIT BOY [*pointing to the streamers*]: So, what do you think, Tanya, are we good?

TANYA: Gorgeous, now I've got to get the table-cloths. And, oh right, the ducks, Krista, come on now.

WAYNE: It's gonna be a real nice day for Miss Ruby.

ZOE: How long have you known her?

WAYNE: Oh god, since the beginning of time.

SISSY NA NA [*to* TANYA]: I'll do the tablecloths—they're in this bag, right?

[SISSY NA NA *starts singing here, singing underneath the rest of this dialogue.*]

KRISTA: Yeah, yeah, yeah . . .

TANYA: She's gonna love it when she sees them, she's gonna light up.

ZOE: Has she lived here long?

WAYNE: She's lived here twenty-five years.

ZOE: No way.

WAYNE [*to* SISSY NA NA, *regarding the song lyrics*]: It's *blame*, not *bang*.

[*Back to* ZOE:] It was almost fashionable, the Hummingbird, when she moved in.

BAIT BOY: What about Cokes?

TANYA: Oh right, yes, we need more—could you pick some up?

KRISTA: And Cheetos. I ate all the Cheetos.

TANYA: Krista, I love you, but you don't make it easy.

Your daddy lets you drink beer?

ZOE: He's not my daddy.

WAYNE: Well then!

SISSY NA NA [*stopping singing for a moment to speak*]: Tanya, you picked up the Chanel? The Chanel No. 5? (She loves her Chanel.)

[SISSY NA NA *and* TERRY *resume singing*.]

ZOE: Because I am sixteen and I am at the *Hummingbird*.

WAYNE: There ya go, dawlin'. Have a beer, it's Jazz Fest.

TANYA [*responding to* SISSY NA NA]: Yes, yes, of course, I got it, I got everything . . .

BAIT BOY [*to* ZOE]: You can have one. Because you are sixteen and in New Orleans.

TANYA: That's right, baby, you are at the *Hummingbird*, and we may be a little rough around the edges, but if there is one thing we know how to do, it is throw down a party.

[BAIT BOY *gives a "yip yip!"*]

That's right, it's Jazz Fest and our dear friend is sunsetting and needs to be celebrated. Because people don't celebrate enough in this life—

ZOE: What does Jazz Fest have to do with anything?

WAYNE: It's like, uh . . . a season, a special time.

TERRY: Amen.

TANYA: They let things roll by unnoticed, which is why it's

SISSY NA NA [*responding to* TANYA]: All right.

good you are doing your little paper, sweetie—don't let Sissy Na Na scare you, you are a good little student, we're glad you decided to come out here and notice us.

I mean, how would this city *survive* without us?

BAIT BOY: Who dat!

TANYA: Who's gonna serve those belligerent frat boys drinks?

Who's gonna make sure the whole slutty bachelorette party gets up onstage for the booty dance?

Who's gonna serve the half-drunk housewife from Charlotte Sex on the Beach out of a test tube you are holding in your cleavage?

[*To* ZOE:]
Celebrate, you hear me?

'Cause we had to go down a long strange road to be who we are—

[*She points to* KRISTA *and then* WAYNE.]

You know. You know. A road filled with construction and

ZOE [*responding to* TANYA, *a little confused*]: Oh, right, thanks.

[SISSY NA NA *growls at* ZOE.]

WAYNE [*raising a glass*]: Here, here.

SISSY NA NA: Lord help me . . .

Bait Boy . . .

roadkill and booby traps and scam artists and bad decisions masquerading as good decisions and bad luck masquerading as good luck and bad friends masquerading as good friends and treachery lurking around every corner, and you just stay on the road—

Looking for an exit, and when you realize there is no exit, you get out and start walking—

You start walking and you keep walking, along the edge of the highway, with no idea of where you're going or where you belong. Until one morning the sun rises and you find yourself here. And there is no one else like us in the whole world. Yes we are.

BAIT BOY: Zoe, come on, let's get the Cokes and I'll take you to City Park.

ZOE: BAIT BOY:
   Wait.   Come on.

SISSY NA NA [*responding to* TANYA]: Yes.

[ZOE *and* BAIT BOY *kind of stand near the office listening to* TANYA *with* WAYNE.]

[*A moment passes.* TANYA *is winded; this rant has taken her someplace she did not expect to go.*]

BAIT BOY: Well, all right. See you guys in a bit.

[BAIT BOY *and* ZOE *leave.* SISSY NA NA *gives* TANYA *a big kiss on the cheek.*]

TANYA: Good-bye.

WAYNE: Bye.

KRISTA: Sissy, can I come use your makeup?

SISSY NA NA: Come on.

[KRISTA *follows* SISSY NA NA *up to her room.*]

TANYA: Was he going to get Cokes?

WAYNE: He's got it. Underneath all that other stuff, Bait Boy is a dependable guy.

TANYA: Well, I guess I better go get cleaned up.

[TANYA *heads upstairs.*]

WAYNE: Hang on tight, Tanya.

TANYA [*as she walks, not looking back*]: I am. Thank you, really.

[TANYA *walks to her room, opens the door, and goes inside.*]

[WAYNE *pours himself a beer from the keg.*]

WAYNE: Where'd you get this keg, Terry?

TERRY: Somebody owed me a favor.

[WAYNE *takes a sip,* TERRY *looks out into the distance. We hear muted music, maybe coming from a car radio. James Booker singing "Junco Partner."*]

Mr. Wayne, I noticed this railing is a little loose / over there on the other side. I think I'm gonna go in your supply closet—I know, but someone could really hurt themselves, so I'm gonna just go look over there in the closet and see what I can find. Don't want nobody to get hurt at Miss Ruby's party.

WAYNE: Yeah, it's been like that for years . . .

[*The music gets closer and* FRANCIS *bikes up. The music is coming out of his fanny pack.*]

What the—

FRANCIS: I know, isn't it remarkable?

TERRY: That's ridiculous.

FRANCIS: I got it from this kid, this kid who runs this, I don't know, culture vulture website—I don't know, I don't go on the inter-web—and I put up some flyers for him and helped fix his cable, and he paid me with this. It's called the jammy pack. Listen!

[*They listen to Booker for a minute.*]

Booker, man. Rest in peace. To be a gay, black, one-eyed heroin-addicted piano genius in 1975 . . .

WAYNE: In New Orleans. In New Orleans in 1975.

[FRANCIS *takes boxes of crackers out of his bag; they seem a little banged up like they have been taken on a road trip and then put back in the pantry.*]

FRANCIS: Hey, listen, I got these crackers, two boxes of crackers, and I'm thinking that's good, right? / I mean these will be good with salsa, this one's got—flax or whatever—and lime. Do you think? I think it's fine . . .

WAYNE: I'm sure that's fine, I mean it's not fancy salsa. It'll be . . . it's gonna be about the people anyway.

[*Beat.* TANYA *opens her door. She's got her hair pulled back and maybe cold cream on her face.*]

TANYA: Three bags of tortilla chips, Frannie. Three bags, *three bags*! Do it for Miss Ruby, goddamn it, do it!

[TANYA *slams the door.*]

FRANCIS: But Tanya, look at these crackers!

[WAYNE *and* FRANCIS *look at each other like, "Well, what are you going to do?" During the following exchange* WAYNE *goes into the office to get the cash for* FRANCIS. *Both men keep talking the whole time, even when* WAYNE *is in the office; they don't stop until* WAYNE *hands him the cash. Also during this exchange* TERRY *slips into the supply closet, turns on the light, and steps in, to look for supplies. The door slowly closes behind him, or at least enough for him to not really be present.* WAYNE *does not notice.*]

FRANCIS: So Wayne, ya think you could hit me up with a five spot so I can get these chips? I mean I don't want Tanya on my ass, not today, no. Remember I gave you back twenty-five at the St. Patrick's parade, and they haven't given me many hours at the record store. I mean, the crackers would have been fine, they're fine in there, it's just the box, the box is messed up—do you know how much food

WAYNE: Yeah sure, why not, of course no problem, I mean it just means your tab is up to, like, a hundred and fifty, but it's gonna be a nice party, we wanna make it nice—where'd you get those crackers anyway? It looks like someone slept on them. Oh God, another party at the Hummingbird. Well, it's been a while anyway, and the last one, the last one wrapped up by three A.M. and resulted in no injuries, all players

gets thrown away each day in New Orleans? In the United States? Tortilla chips, I never even knew tortilla chips existed until, like, I think 1989, and now it's all Frito-Lay bullshit, tortilla chips. I'm just against them, I am against tortilla chips unless you are in Mexico and some seventy-five-year-old grandma is making them by hand especially for you in her thatched hut or whatever, *then* I will eat a frikken tortilla chip—hey thanks, really, thanks.

All right, let me go do this.

Don't worry, I got my helmet. And the jammy pack!

remained on the field! I don't care what anybody says, Miss Ruby is a *gem*, that woman does not have a mean bone in her body. Any bad things that happened have happened out of *love*, she just has too much *love* in her, it blinds her to all the what, ramifications: she is blinded by love for the human race. Here man, this is for *tortilla chips*, you hear?

All right. Be careful on that bike.

[WAYNE *watches* FRANCIS *bike off, then turns around. Perhaps he sits in his chair?*]

WAYNE: The thing is, Terry—when I think about my dad and his dad and his dad, nobody was really trying to hurt me. When my great-grandfather opened the hat shop, I wasn't anywhere on the horizon. He couldn't think about how maybe, just maybe I would have been a great milliner, if given the chance. But what did he know—I could have been born with two gimp legs or a rare blood condition. I could have been born a girl, a deaf girl, and a deaf girl can't really take over a hat shop, can she? There was no way my great-grandfather could anticipate the chain of events that would lead me to becoming the worst fucking air-conditioner repairman in the history of the universe, and to me knowing that was true, and to my dad knowing that was true, and to that day in the middle of August when we both knew I had to strike out on my own. Hey what time is it, anyway?

[WAYNE *looks around, realizes* TERRY *is gone.*]

Aw, look at me, I'm talking to myself.

[*He raises his glass to no one in particular.*]

Cheers.

[WAYNE *shuffles into his office. For a moment, the courtyard of the Hummingbird Hotel stands alone, settling just a half a hair into the wet earth below.*]

[*Blackout.*]

ACT 2

SCENE 1

[*Several hours later, maybe three thirty or four in the afternoon. The party is in full swing. All the major characters are in the middle of singing "Little Liza Jane," which erupted out of nowhere maybe three minutes before.* KRISTA *sits on the roof of the car with her legs hanging down over the windshield.* BAIT BOY *is three and a half beers under and a little sweaty, his pants dirty from wiping his hands on them, his shirt untucked with one button undone. He sings near the car with* KRISTA. ZOE *and* TANYA *stand near each other, maybe near the buffet table, which is full of the whole spread—except the tortilla chips. Also a couple random bottles of booze that people have brought as offerings.* TERRY *is near the keg, singing and pouring himself a beer.* WAYNE *holds court near the office, sitting in his chair near the door.* SISSY NA NA *is on the upstairs walkway, singing to the group.*

There may be a few more decorations up. And there are puffy yellow paper party ducks everywhere—*on the tables, on the ground, on the car, taped to the banisters.*

Everyone is in some version of festive New Orleans carnival attire. SISSY NA NA *is the most decked out: a big pink or purple wig, glittery* false eyelashes, gold glitter hot pants with a bustle tied on in the back, a halter top that shows off fake boobs, glittery jewelry. TANYA wears a festive dress with a cheap purple boa around her neck, a feather in her hair, and a cheap glittery pink half mask. KRISTA has painted her face with colorful face-paint designs and wears some kind of sparkly dress, colorful stockings, and boots. Someone let BAIT BOY borrow their plastic fake butt and glitter sunglasses in the shape of stars. WAYNE has on a T-shirt from Mardi Gras 1995 and some old carnival beads he found. Someone has planted a big kiss on his forehead, leaving the lipstick mark, and TANYA or SISSY NA NA has put one giant clip-on earring on one of his ears and tied a woman's scarf around his neck. ZOE has pulled a purple ballerina tutu up over her jeans, has Mardi Gras beads wrapped around her wrist, wears a tiara, and has a couple of face decorations that KRISTA painted on her. TERRY wears one of SISSY NA NA's bobbed wigs, his "Katrina, You Bitch" T-shirt, and a drugstore hula skirt pulled up over his jeans.

There are dozens of PARTY GUESTS at the funeral, who might include burlesque dancers who used to work for MISS RUBY, MISS RUBY's old next-door neighbors before she moved to the Hummingbird, hipster artists, and people who have visited her club over the years. It's likely we only see seven or so of these new guests on stage; they should be a mix of ages and races. These guests are scattered about the stage, in the parking lot, on the stairs, on the balcony. Most of them sing with the group, although at least one pocket of people is just smoking and having a conversation as the others sing. During the song some people come up to the keg and get a beer, singing the whole time.]

	Oh, Eliza, little Liza Jane. Oh, Eliza, little Liza Jane ... Oh, Eliza, little Liza Jane. Oh, Eliza, little Liza Jane ...
[FRANCIS bikes into the party. As the song continues, FRANCIS takes two bags of tortilla chips out of	

his bag and dances with them over to TANYA *and* ZOE. *He gives* TANYA *a big hug, and* ZOE *takes the chips out of his hands while he is hugging* TANYA. ZOE *puts the chips in a bowl as* TANYA *seems to be speaking harshly to* FRANCIS. FRANCIS *is like, "Don't worry, don't worry" and whistles loudly to* PARTY GUEST ONE *on the balcony.* PARTY GUEST ONE *waves hello and reaches down into his or her backpack.* PARTY GUEST ONE *throws a third bag of tortilla chips down to* FRANCIS. TANYA *shakes her head and laughs as* FRANCIS *dances his way over to* TANYA, *maybe doing a little bow before her as he hands her the tortilla chips.* TANYA *laughs, takes the chips, and slaps his behind as he dances away.*]

SISSY NA NA: Hey, little girl, would you tell me your name?
[ALL: *Little Liza Jane*]
If I love you baby, would you feel the same?
[ALL: *Little Liza Jane*]

Oh, Eliza, little Liza Jane. Oh, Eliza, little Liza Jane . . .
Oh, Eliza, little Liza Jane. Oh, Eliza, little Liza Jane . . .

[*Perhaps* SISSY NA NA *has danced downstairs. She pushes* BAIT BOY *to the center. He dances while she sings.*]

Oh, Eliza, little Liza Jane. Oh, Eliza, little Liza Jane . . .
Oh, Eliza, little Liza Jane. Oh, Eliza, little Liza Jane . . .

BAIT BOY: One two three four five six seven
[ALL: *Little Liza Jane*]
Can ya dance, Miss Ruby, right into heaven?
[ALL: *Little Liza Jane*]

Oh, Eliza, little Liza Jane. Oh, Eliza, little Liza Jane . . .
Oh, Eliza, little Liza Jane. Oh, Eliza, little Liza Jane . . .

[*Suddenly, the gutter pipe that* TERRY *fixed in act 1 comes crashing down in one big thud. There are two or three* PARTY GUESTS *on the upstairs walkway, near where it falls; they scatter as it swings down. Everyone gasps, and the song peters out. The overlapping of the following lines will vary from production to production.*]

TERRY: Oh, lord.

[TERRY *runs up the stairs to where the gutter pipe fell, followed by* WAYNE.]

TANYA: Is everyone okay?

WAYNE [*speaking in kind of an evolving roar*]: TEEEEEERR-RRRRYYYYYY! I knew you didn't use those screws, Terry! You returned those screws and kept the moncy, didn't you, you did, didn't you?

KRISTA: Oh my god, that scared the shit out of me.

TERRY: I did, I did use those screws, I swear, Mr. Wayne, you can't see them, they stuck up in the roofline—

WAYNE: What if someone had been standing there?

PARTY GUEST ONE [*speaking after* WAYNE *says "kept the money"*]: What happened?

[*To someone standing nearby*]

PARTY GUEST TWO: The gutter pipe fell.

Are you okay?

ZOE: But what happened?

TERRY: I'll do it again, Mr. Wayne, I'll do it again *for free*—I try, I really do, I just needed the money right then . . .

BAIT BOY: I don't know, it just fell.

PARTY GUEST ONE: That could have killed someone.

WAYNE: *Exactly*, now you're going to have to waste time doing it again for *free*.

[WAYNE *is now near the gutter pipe; he reaches to pick it up, then stops.*]

Jesus! This gutter pipe is so old we really should replace the whole thing.

TERRY: That's what I'm saying! I could have used astronaut nails and that gutter pipe woulda still fallen down!

WAYNE: Why didn't you tell me that this morning?

[WAYNE *and* TERRY *kind of try to move the gutter pipe. It's awkward, and the gutter pipe is sharp.*]

[*Having cut his finger*] Ow! Ow! Shit!

PARTY GUEST TWO: I know.

[BAIT BOY *heads up to where the accident happened.*]

BAIT BOY: Is everyone okay up here?

FRANCIS [*singing*]: Nooooo . . . it ain't my fault . . .

TANYA [*to* WAYNE]: *This is so typical, Wayne!* Typical!

SISSY NA NA [*to* TANYA]: Don't you worry about that—

TANYA: Now all everybody's going to talk about is the goddamn gutter pipe!

[SISSY NA NA *gets an idea.*]

SISSY NA NA: Hold on.

[SISSY NA NA *runs up the stairs to get the Irish Car Bombs.*]

TERRY: I think we better leave it right here, it's not safe—

WAYNE: Yeah, you're probably right (shit).

TERRY [*announcing*]: Nobody come around this area right here, all right! Stay away from this gutter pipe area!

TANYA: Jesus, Francis, get me a beer . . .

PARTY GUEST ONE: Oh wait, I think my arm is cut, wait, my arm.

BAIT BOY: Let me see.

PARTY GUEST TWO: That's not blood, that's just ketchup or something.

PARTY GUEST ONE: No, I think . . . oh yeah, I guess it is ketchup, but that's weird, I didn't eat anything with ketchup on it.

BAIT BOY: You're okay?

PARTY GUEST TWO: He's fine.

BAIT BOY: Okay.

SISSY NA NA [*while going into her room*]: Get ready, Bait Boy!

[BAIT BOY *is like, huh?*]

[FRANCIS *brings* TANYA *a beer. A man in his seventies walks toward* MISS RUBY's *door.*]

TANYA [*whispering to* FRANCIS]: Oh my god, that's Judge Harmon—
good afternoon, Judge!

JUDGE HARMON: Oh, hello there Tanya.

TANYA: Thank you for coming, you hear? It means a lot to her, you hear?

JUDGE HARMON: Of course. She taught me a thing or two over the years.

TANYA: I'm sure she did.

[BAIT BOY *has been talking to the girls upstairs.*]

[JUDGE HARMON *enters* MISS RUBY's *room.*]

PARTY GUEST ONE: You still work in the Quarter?

TANYA [*to* FRANCIS]: And people said she had no influence.

BAIT BOY: No, I moved to Atlanta.

PARTY GUEST TWO: You miss it here?

BAIT BOY: Nah—

PARTY GUEST TWO: Come on!

BAIT BOY: All right, all right. I miss . . .

[*Maybe* BAIT BOY *closes his eyes.*]

K-Doe and Antoinette crashing Galactic's Cozy Corner gig to sing "Here Come the Girls."

PARTY GUEST ONE [*like, yes, nothing like it*]: Uh! Come on, keep it coming.

BAIT BOY: I miss . . . Moose—stopping by the club every night at three A.M. when he finished his shift at the Clover Grill. And then getting word about four A.M. breakfast at Elaine's house over on Dauphine, a beautiful mix of people—black, white, millionaires, flat-broke losers like Francis, putting the Meters on the record player and dancing, always dancing.

PARTY GUEST TWO: Yeah, you miss it here, hoss.

BAIT BOY: Well, it was too much for me, I had to get out, but there was this feeling of . . . of . . .

FRANCIS: Bacchanal, man, bacchanal, boundaries out the window, panoramic bliss—
fat man down the street smokes reefer
to ease pain,
people sleep dreaming rhythm
(bass rhythm)

[TANYA *busies herself cleaning up trash around the sandwich table, maybe refreshing the chips.*]

FRANCIS [*after* BAIT BOY *says* "*Moose*"]: Mooooooooooose.

TANYA: Oh, poor Elaine!

FRANCIS [*responding to* BAIT BOY]: Hey!

KRISTA: It really could be beautiful.

ZOE [*to* KRISTA]: Is he a poet?

KRISTA: Yeah. He's pretty good . . .

or sit with their thoughts,
ooh poo pa doo (another day),
they call us *all* the most.

[*Maybe a few people clap, maybe
someone twirls* BAIT BOY *around
or fake punches him or just does
some other dumbass move.* PARTY
GUESTS ONE *and* TWO *together
yell, "Three* A.M. *breakdown!"
And three people do a minidance,*
BAIT BOY's *three* A.M. *dance.* BAIT
BOY *is like, "No, man, no, not
going there."*]

FRANCIS: Bacchanal, man, it's a
    spiritual thing,
    a cleansing, an opening up to
    the libido—

[FRANCIS *points at his groin and
gives a little pump.*]

—the libido, don't be scared.

[*He points at his groin again and
gives a little pump.*]

Don't be scared.

[*He gives another little pump.*]

PARTY GUEST ONE: Hey Bait Boy,
    remember how you would
    bait the crowd with that
    song . . . *da-na-na-na*?

BAIT BOY: That's what you call a
   karaoke cocktease!

[*There is a burst of laughter near*
BAIT BOY.]

[SISSY NA NA *comes out of her
room with a tray holding a bottle
of Irish whiskey, two Guinness
beers, two beer glasses, and two
shot glasses. Does she bring this
downstairs? Or is there a table on
the balcony she can use?*]

SISSY NA NA: All right, everybody, everybody, can I have your attention, please, can I have your—*if you can hear me, say, "Hell,
   yeah"!*

[*Some people say, "Hell, yeah."*]

   If you can hear me, say, "Shit goddamn, yeah"!

[*More people say, "Shit goddamn, yeah."*]

   If you can hear me, say, "Sissy Na Na for president"!

[*Pretty much everyone says, "Sissy Na Na for president," and she has
everyone's attention.*]

   Hello and welcome to the living funeral for the one and only
   Miss Ruby!

[*There are hoots and hollers at different points throughout her following speech.*]

We'd like to thank our host, Mr. Wayne Murphy—

[*Cheers.*]

For opening the doors of his kingdom for this celebration—

[WAYNE *bows a flamboyant bow, and perhaps there is a shout or two of "All hail!" or "King Wayne!"*]

And to the esteemed Miss Tanya, for organizing private visits and the food . . .

[*A couple of hoots and hollers are offered as* TANYA *waves.*]

We are gathered here today to honor the angel who looks upon you all with an utterly nonjudgmental eye—the drunks, the addicts, the ex-addicts—

[*A few cheers and snaps.*]

—the ho's, the superho's, the ex-cons, the soon-to-be cons, the bouncers, the strippers, the street musicians, the faggots, the poets, the activists, the dykes, the trannies, the supertrannies— whoop whoop! Those who are forgotten and the general down-and-out. Miss Ruby welcomes you all.

[*More cheers.*]

If you need to repent, she will show you how. If you need a good spanking, well, she can take care of that too.

And this day has *also* brought back some of our most infamous scoundrels. Bait Boy, Bait Boy, Bait Boy . . .

[BAIT BOY *kind of shakes his head as everyone chants and cheers.*]

You promised!

[*Chanting*]

Get ready, get ready, take your pants off, / take your pants off—

PARTY GUEST TWO [*aside*]: Why do you have to take your pants off?

BAIT BOY [*to* SISSY NA NA]: Did you do the interview yet?

SISSY NA NA: Not yet, but I will, don't worry. Come on over here.

[SISSY NA NA *pours two glasses of Guinness and two shots of whiskey for her and* BAIT BOY.]

Bait Boy, your presence conjures so many memories: who remembers the Lundi Gras night when Bait Boy told those frat boys he could get them some meth, and took the money in advance?

BAIT BOY: Cover your ears, Zoe!

ZOE: I don't care.

[*Everyone is like, awwwww!*]

[KRISTA *kind of covers* ZOE's *ears;* ZOE *shrugs her off.*]

All I can say about that night is that it's a good thing my daddy taught this girl how to knife fight!

Anyhoo, Bait Boy, seems you're reformed now, and in the spirit of Miss Ruby, we forgive you.

BAIT BOY: Come on now, Sissy, I wasn't—

SISSY NA NA: We forgive you for *everything*, and we are happy to know that you have not abandoned us, and that now we can reach out to *you* when we are in need.

[*Is* BAIT BOY *maybe a little startled by this prospect?*]

BAIT BOY: Of course, anytime, of course.

SISSY NA NA: An Irish Car Bomb
    for our favorite Irishman—   FRANCIS: Hey what about me!

BAIT BOY: I'm not Irish.

SISSY NA NA: —Bait Boy!

[SISSY NA NA *and* BAIT BOY *do the Irish Car Bombs. Lots of cheering, then dispersing into different party conversation groups. During* BAIT BOY *and* SISSY NA NA'*s conversation,* TANYA *makes her way to a photo album that sits near a guest book sign in. So does* TERRY. WAYNE *eventually settles down into the chair by his office, and maybe one of the female* PARTY GUESTS *comes and sits on his knee.* FRANCIS *brings another* PARTY GUEST *around the corner to smoke a joint.*]

BAIT BOY [*pushing* SISSY NA NA *or messing with her hair*]: Why you calling me out, Sissy?

SISSY NA NA: Stop that.

BAIT BOY: Why you calling me out?

SISSY NA NA: Because you need to remember where you came from.

BAIT BOY: Oh, I remember. You taking my hand, sneaking me out the back door of the bar and into the streets.

SISSY NA NA: I was a mess back then, didn't know my left from my right—

BAIT BOY: Walking all the way down the levee in the midnight air to the party at the house with all the closets—remember those closets, Sissy?

[*Does* BAIT BOY *try to touch* SISSY NA NA's *hair?*]

SISSY NA NA [*shaking him off*]: I would like you to take your hands off me, please—

BAIT BOY: Hey now, go easy, don't be a stress case.

SISSY NA NA: I would like you to take your hands off me, please.

[*Does* BAIT BOY *laugh? Does he do a little chant from the old days? "Sissy Sissy Na Na, Sissy Sissy Na Na."*]

TANYA [*pointing to the photo album*]: Oh my god, Terry, is that you?

[*The photograph isn't visible, but it is like a younger* TERRY *in a glittery vest and hot pants.*]

TERRY: It is. Miss Ruby put me in one of her routines once.

TANYA: What on earth are you wearing!

TERRY: Anything for that woman, anything.

[*They continue looking at the photo album. Eventually* TERRY *makes his way toward* WAYNE, *and* TANYA *makes her way to the sandwich table.*]

SISSY NA NA [*to* BAIT BOY]: You know what I fucking *hated* about the way you ran the stage at Cat's Meow?

BAIT BOY: What?

SISSY NA NA: You never *actually* let anybody karaoke. You were in it for your *own* fun.

BAIT BOY: I had that place packed wall-to-wall, even on a Wednesday. I was legendary.

[SISSY NA NA *gets real close to* BAIT BOY.]

SISSY NA NA: Why are you here?

BAIT BOY: To say good-bye. I want Miss Ruby to see how good I'm doing, so she can die in peace.

SISSY NA NA: And on the eighth day, God created Bait Boy!

BAIT BOY: Jealousy makes you look old, Sissy.

SISSY NA NA: Don't you ruin this, motherfucker. This day is about more than just you.

[SISSY NA NA *walks away, up the stairs, and into* MISS RUBY's *room. Let's say* BAIT BOY *hangs with some other* PARTY GUESTS. KRISTA *walks up to* ZOE, *who is either watching the party or typing on her iPad.*]

KRISTA: So Bait Boy never mentioned me to you?

ZOE: Well, I mean, he talked about *all* of you.

KRISTA: Right.

ZOE: So how long have you been working as a paralegal?

KRISTA: A what?

ZOE: Isn't that what you told Greg—

KRISTA: Oh right, yeah, sorry, I forgot, 'cause, you know, I just got my certificate.

ZOE: From a school? Is there a paralegal school or something?

KRISTA: Yeah, they gave me a certificate in a silver frame.

ZOE: But back then—

KRISTA: Back when I was living here, I was a dancer at Babe's.

ZOE: And Babe's is a—

KRISTA: A strip club, sweetie. In the Quarter.

ZOE: Okay.

[ZOE *types on her iPad. A burst of laughter from* FRANCIS *with another group of guests, and maybe the following line is sung: "What's her name? Can't tell you—nooo."* WAYNE *is talking to* PARTY GUESTS *and eventually to* TERRY.]

WAYNE: So look, the restaurant was right in that room right there—see that boarded-up window? There was food, cocktails, dancing . . .

TERRY: My grandma used to work there, she worked the bathroom.

PARTY GUEST ONE: You mean like cleaning the bathroom?

TERRY: No, like handing out mints and hand towels.

PARTY GUEST TWO: It was that fancy?

WAYNE: It was that fancy. And all it needs is a little TLC.

TERRY: Well—

WAYNE: I'm serious.

ZOE [*to* KRISTA]: I bet you made good money.

KRISTA: Well, the real money comes if you get your customer up to the Champagne Room. That costs a grand, and the girl gets forty percent. But, you know, sometimes it's two girls that get the guy up there, and then there's a split . . .

ZOE: And what happens in the Champagne Room?

KRISTA: That's confidential.

ZOE: Oh well, I won't put it in the paper.

KRISTA: How old are you?

ZOE: Sixteen. But that's like forty-five in Google years.

KRISTA [*laughing a little*]: All right.

[KRISTA *leans over and whispers for a while in* ZOE'*s ear.* SISSY NA NA *runs out of* MISS RUBY'*s room.*]

TERRY: What you need is some capital.

WAYNE: Ah come on, whatever happened to elbow grease?

SISSY NA NA [*calling*]: Tanya. *Tanya!*

TANYA: What?

TERRY: Baby, I think the Chinese bought it all up last year!

[WAYNE *and* TERRY *crack up.*]

SISSY NA NA: She wants to taste a praline.

TANYA: Oh, sweet thing . . .

WAYNE: Maybe I should write the Chinese!

[TANYA *goes to the stairs and meets* SISSY NA NA *halfway or maybe hands it up.*]

[*They laugh.*]

ZOE [*to* KRISTA, *squealing with laughter*]: No!

KRISTA: Yes.

TANYA [*to* SISSY NA NA]: Just a little piece, now, okay? That will dissolve in her mouth.

SISSY NA NA: I know, Tanya, I *know*.

[SISSY NA NA *takes the praline into* MISS RUBY's *room.*]

ZOE: I mean do you, like, train for that?

KRISTA: Ah, you learn quick. They're very simple creatures, really.

WAYNE [*waving* TERRY *toward the old restaurant*]: Really though, Terry, come on, come see.

TERRY: Nah, last time you took me in there I got an asthma attack.

[TANYA *walks back to the sandwich table and takes just a liiittle bite of one of* BAIT BOY's *sandwiches.*]

TANYA: Bait Boy, these sandwiches taste like something crawled under a house and died.

BAIT BOY: All fancy things taste that way! That's how rich people like it!

[BAIT BOY *grabs* TANYA *and dances with her. Around here, "The Wobble" song is turned on, and the wobble dance begins.*]

FRANCIS [*dancing the line dance, yelling*]: Hey Wayne, I bet it's Bait Boy's wife that's clearing the lot across the street.

ZOE [*kind of calling out, but no one really hears her*]: They're not married!

[*To* KRISTA, *as* BAIT BOY *shoots the bird at* FRANCIS:]

They're not married.

KRISTA: They're not?

ZOE: No, I don't know why everybody keeps saying that.

KRISTA: He must really love her, huh?

ZOE: I think the technical term is pussy whipped.

KRISTA: No shit.

ZOE [*still half typing*]: I tease him about it all the time. Greg and I are really close.

KRISTA: Yeah?

ZOE: Oh yeah, I talk to Greg way more than I talk to my mom.

KRISTA: Does he tell you how pretty you are?

ZOE: What? No!

KRISTA: 'Cause you *are* pretty . . .

ZOE: He's just really supportive.

[KRISTA's *eyes are like, "right."*]

I didn't like him at first, but now I really trust Greg.

KRISTA: That's good, sweetie. You're a lucky girl.

[*Around here,* SISSY NA NA *comes out of* MISS RUBY's *room. She comes down the stairs and joins the wobble dance, or maybe joins a group on the balcony.*]

TANYA: So how are you, Bait Boy, are you happy?

BAIT BOY: Ah, happiness is overrated.

TANYA: But are you happy?

[BAIT BOY *spins* TANYA *hard. She laughs.* FRANCIS *is messing up the wobble.*]

BAIT BOY [*to* FRANCIS]: Frannie, a line dance is about staying *in line*.

TANYA [*still dancing with* BAIT BOY]: We must look like something somebody pulled out of the trash.

BAIT BOY: Nah, nah.

TANYA: A pile of rubbish.

BAIT BOY: Come on, no, y'all are, like—what's that word all the pricey restaurants use now—

TANYA: Organic?

BAIT BOY: No, no.

TANYA: Artisanal?

BAIT BOY: That's it—you all are artisanal.

[TANYA *laughs.*]

KRISTA [*to* ZOE, *watching the crowd dance*]: Look at those idiots.

TANYA: You know, when Miss Ruby dies, I'll be the old one.

BAIT BOY: Ahh . . . come on—

TANYA: It's true!

BAIT BOY: You'll be the glamour queen, watching over us all!

[BAIT BOY *dips* TANYA.]

TANYA: Bait Boy, you sure know how to play a girl . . .

[TERRY *emerges from the wobble dance, dancing up to* ZOE.]

TERRY: Hey Miss Hotlanta, you know how to wobble?

ZOE: Yeah, I mean at weddings . . .

TERRY: Ya can't just listen to people talk, you gotta get in there—
yeah, yeah.

KRISTA: Leave her alone, Terry, she's interviewing me. Right, you're
still interviewing me.

[KRISTA *pushes* TERRY *away, he goes back to dancing.* ZOE *is now film-
ing the dance with her iPhone. The dance has grown, and it has a wild
and wonderful energy.*]

ZOE: How does this happen?

KRISTA: You mean this, like—*this*?

[*She indicates the dance, which is now ending. People clap and cheer
over these next lines.*]

ZOE: Yes.

KRISTA: Oh God . . .

ZOE: Come on . . .

FRANCIS [*emerging from the dance*]: We gonna hoolla tralla walla
malla dalla
drink some mellow wine.

[*He looks into* ZOE's *phone as she films.*]

Sometimes I feel guilty for being happy.

KRISTA [*to* ZOE]: It's like . . . look . . . the first time I ever saw Tanya,
she was sitting on the curb at the corner of Bourbon and Tou-
louse, sitting there in the middle of all the craziness. People
passing her by thinking she's just another drunk. Put my hand on
the top of her head and said, "What's wrong, sweetie?" And she

looks up and says, "My mother died today, and I haven't spoken to her in nine years." Takes my hand—I remember her hand was so cold. And that's how I started knowing Tanya. And I've been knowing her for . . .

[KRISTA *adds up on her fingers.*]

Twelve years now. I don't know what else to say about it . . .

TANYA [*in her own space, assessing what needs to happen next at the party*]: All right, let's see.

ZOE [*to* KRISTA, *reading from her iPad*]: So would you call it a reciprocal relationship of care that binds you together?

KRISTA: I'm sorry?

ZOE: What keeps you guys together?

KRISTA: Who knows? Bad luck. Bad tempers. No bullshit. No pretending.

ZOE: Holy shit.

KRISTA: What?

ZOE: You just gave me a kick-ass title for my paper.

KRISTA: Really?

ZOE: You should be a writer . . .

KRISTA: Let me see that . . .

[KRISTA *kind of looks over* ZOE's *shoulder at* ZOE's *typing.*]

Ah, I don't even know how to type.

[ZOE *keeps typing.*]

Whoa, you're fast.

[TANYA *calls across the party to* SISSY NA NA.]

TANYA: Sissy, you think we should—

SISSY NA NA: Yeah, I'll start gathering some chairs.

ZOE [*to* KRISTA]: Okay, so why did you move out of the
    Hummingbird?

KRISTA: Next question.

ZOE: Come on, I don't care . . .

KRISTA: Wayne kicked me out because I was *four weeks late / on rent,*
    and so I had to go, *right, Wayne?*

WAYNE: It was eight weeks, *eight weeks,* and the first four I paid
    myself / so the owners wouldn't think anything fishy was
    going on—

KRISTA: You'd rather me be out on the street, sleeping in City Park /
    on a park bench than in the Hummingbird Hotel, right, Wayne?

WAYNE: You don't know the kind
    of pressure I'm under, / you
    don't *know* what it takes to
    hold this place together—   TANYA: Hey you two make nice
                                                  MAKE NICE!
KRISTA: You don't know what it
    feels like to be carrying your
    whole life around in a back-
    pack, do you, Wayne?

[WAYNE *waves her off, goes to get a beer.* TANYA *starts helping* SISSY
NA NA *drag chairs into a half circle.*]

ZOE: Oh my God.

KRISTA: What?

ZOE: Are you homeless?

KRISTA: No. What? No. I live with my sister on the Westbank. I live with my sister, I'm putting money away, I, I babysit her kids.

ZOE: Because if you need help—

BAIT BOY: Yeah, Krista, if you need help—

KRISTA: I'm *fine*.

ZOE: Atlanta is booming right now, some of my friends are taking a gap year to work on start-ups before college—

KRISTA: Taking a what?

[*To* BAIT BOY, *irritated and confused:*]

What is she talking about?

BAIT BOY: It's like taking a year off between high school and college—

ZOE: —and my mom, she worked with this life coach—

KRISTA: Life coach?

BAIT BOY: Zoe—

ZOE: —when she was starting her business, and everything just took off! / I mean, maybe you should try Atlanta.

KRISTA: Listen, it's nice that you're here, but you don't know anything about us, and we don't *need your help*. If there's one thing this group of people *knows* how to *do*, it is *help themselves*—

ZOE: No no no I was just—

KRISTA: —because *we know* that nobody is going to *magically swoop down from Atlanta* and save us.

[BAIT BOY *is trying to pull* KRISTA *away.*]

BAIT BOY: Krista, sweetie, calm down.

KRISTA: Oh, except for maybe *one* of us who gets some magic fucking fairy dust—magic *Joyce* dust—sprinkled on them, and *poof*, new life, new house, new *heart*, even a *heart of gold*, which is *not* the heart I *knew*—

TERRY [*to* KRISTA]: Baby doll, stop it, he's not worth it—

KRISTA: No, Terry, no—

[*To* ZOE:] We were together for six years, Zoe. *Six years.*

ZOE: What?

KRISTA: Two of them we spent right there in room 107. Did he tell you that? Did you tell her that, Bait Boy?

ZOE: Jesus, Greg.

BAIT BOY: I was gonna tell you—

KRISTA [*to* ZOE]: I *know* him, *you* don't.

BAIT BOY [*taking* KRISTA *in his arms*]: Hey now, hey now.

KRISTA: I know you, she doesn't know you, I do! She's a little bitch, Bait Boy.

BAIT BOY: She's a kid—

KRISTA: She's a catty bitch—

BAIT BOY: Krista, you know that's not true.

ZOE [*to* WAYNE]: I didn't mean to upset her.

TANYA [*to* ZOE]: Sweetness, come over here, forget about them, come here.

WAYNE: Come on, come on, help Uncle Wayne get some ice from the machine. Come on.

WAYNE [*walking* ZOE *to the ice machine*]: No, no . . .

KRISTA: I know, it's me, it's me that's a catty bitch.

BAIT BOY: That's not true either. Hey, hey.

[BAIT BOY *is cradling* KRISTA.]

TANYA [*to the* PARTY GUESTS]: Okay, here we go! I need everyone who considers themselves a lady to come here to the center.

FRANCIS [*being a stupid ass, faking a high voice*]: I'm a lady.

TANYA: Shut up, Francis, you are all man.

FRANCIS: Thank you, dawlin'.

TANYA: Not a compliment.

BAIT BOY [*to* KRISTA]: You are a beautiful person.

KRISTA: You are too. We were like magic.

SISSY NA NA [*aside to* TANYA, *while moving chairs*]: They were like poison.

TANYA: Come on, let's go! Krista!

SISSY NA NA: Let me get a drum.

BAIT BOY [*calling her an old pet name from the early days*]: Hey— Stupid Girl, look at me.

KRISTA: Don't call me that, it makes me sad.

TANYA [*calling to* ZOE, *who is coming back from the ice machine*]: Zoe, get over here, you got lady parts, don't you?

SISSY NA NA [*to* ZOE]: The girls are gonna sing a song to Miss Ruby, and so we're gonna practice.

TANYA [*trying to get* KRISTA *to join the group*]: Krista!

BAIT BOY [*to* KRISTA]: You always wanted to work at a law firm. And now look: you're working at a law firm.

KRISTA: I am not. I am not doing good, and neither are you.

TANYA: Krista!

[*To* TANYA]

What!

TANYA: Come *here. Now.* And sing with us.

KRISTA [*back to* BAIT BOY]: I know you, Bait Boy. Me.

[SISSY NA NA *has found a trash can or something to beat on. The women settle into a half circle around* SISSY NA NA. SISSY NA NA *and* TANYA *quietly explain how the song will work to the women.* WAYNE *has drifted toward the edge of the party and is looking at the Costco.* FRANCIS *joins him.*]

FRANCIS: Did you see what they're doing to the old Frostop? Building a second story, with a slanty roof and a skylight. They say it's gonna be a spa.

WAYNE: A spa?

FRANCIS: That's what I heard.

WAYNE [*declaring like a king*]: The day a spa opens on Airline Highway I will dance naked through the streets!

FRANCIS: Please, Wayne, mercy, mercy . . .

[BAIT BOY *joins* WAYNE *and* FRANCIS. TERRY *is nearby or joins them.*]

BAIT BOY [*referring to the thing with* KRISTA]: So fucking intense . . .

FRANCIS [*handing over his beer to* BAIT BOY]: Here.

WAYNE [*to* BAIT BOY]: That woman is a handful and a half.

FRANCIS [*to* BAIT BOY]: Did you see that? A frikken *Costco*.

BAIT BOY: Well, maybe the people that rent rooms here can go shopping over there . . .

WAYNE: Never gonna happen. Everything at Costco is megasized.

TERRY: And you have to have a / membership.

WAYNE: Regulations, ordinances . . .

FRANCIS: I know—what if you just want *one* roll of toilet paper or something.

BAIT BOY: I know, but look at that, how do you fight that?

FRANCIS [*to* BAIT BOY]: So does Joyce have a really big house or whatever?

BAIT BOY: Yeah, it's nice. She works hard.

FRANCIS: Garage door openers. An alarm system with a code. A lawn.

[BAIT BOY *kind of shrugs, like "yeah." Maybe* FRANCIS *imitates Joyce:*]

"Don't forget to mow the lawn."

TERRY: Always knew you were sniffing that out—

FRANCIS [*to* BAIT BOY]: How can you take it?

BAIT BOY [*to* FRANCIS]: It's not bad, man, I need structure—

[SISSY NA NA *or one of the women in the circle starts a slow, steady drum beat.*]

FRANCIS: You sprung from this ground right here, we don't bury all our dirty stuff under the pavement—

BAIT BOY: —the job, the house, the kid, it's all, it's good for me—

FRANCIS: —can't do it, can't even try. The ground busts right up—

BAIT BOY: This is me. This is who I am.

FRANCIS: —through the sidewalks, through the parking lots, the streets.

BAIT BOY: Shut the fuck up, Francis, I mean, where are you living now?

FRANCIS: I'm living.

BAIT BOY: But where are you living?

[FRANCIS *reaches his arms out from his sides.*]

FRANCIS: I'm free.

[SISSY NA NA *and the women begin to sing their version of Nina Simone's song, "Be My Husband," while the women drum and shake tambourines. They sing the refrain together, and either customize the verses or invent new ones.* ZOE *is in the circle, but does not sing at first.*]

SISSY NA NA:
    Be my husband man I be your wife . . .

[*Verse continues.*]

ALL THE WOMEN [*except* ZOE, *joining in the refrain*]:
    Oh daddy, love me good . . .

[*Refrain continues.*]

[TANYA *sings the second verse, adapting it to, "If you want me to I'll cook and sew / and if I don't want to, I'll just say no," and again all the women sing the refrain, this time with* ZOE *joining in.*]

[KRISTA *turns and sings to* BAIT BOY, *possibly even moving away from the group of women to focus on him.*]

KRISTA [*singing to* BAIT BOY]:
    Feed me chocolate and lick my toes,
    Feed me chocolate and lick my toes,
    Feed me chocolate and lick my toes,
    Stay away from those other ho's.

[*Perhaps* TANYA *gently moves* KRISTA *back to the group, as all the women sing the refrain.*]

ZOE [*taking a solo*]:
    Don't you call me your sweet little girl,
    Don't you call me your sweet little girl,
    Don't you call me your sweet little girl,
    I'll see you when I'm done traveling the world!

[*Everyone hoots and hollers for* ZOE.]

[TERRY *jumps in as the refrain is sung again. The women kind of protest and mock him, but they let him sing. He sings directly to* KRISTA.]

TERRY:
    Don't you make me come beg to you,
    Don't you make me come beggin' to you,
    Don't you make me come beg to you,
    I will build you a house when you ask me to.

[*After a final refrain, the song ends, and everyone at the party claps and cheers.*]

BAIT BOY: Look at little Zoe!

ZOE: Oh God, am I blushing?

TANYA: Yes you are, sugar!

ZOE: Do you all sing like this all the time?

WAYNE: People sing a lot here, I don't know why.

TANYA: Not all the time. I don't know why we do it, I mean, some people watch TV, we sing.

FRANCIS:	BAIT BOY:
I'd rather sing!	I can't sing for shit.

KRISTA: You can sing, Bait Boy.

TANYA: You can sing, Bait Boy, anybody can sing.

ZOE: The only singing I've ever done really was in church—

[SISSY NA NA *grabs* KRISTA, *pulling her away from the crowd.*]

KRISTA: Sissy, God!

TANYA: You just gotta let it out, it's like therapy. Let it all hang out.

ZOE: Like group therapy . . .

TANYA: Or maybe just a few minutes of escape.

ZOE: *Yes.*

[ZOE *retreives her iPad to take notes. During these lines the* PARTY GUESTS *disperse into different party activities—getting drinks, sitting in small groups and talking; maybe* WAYNE *changes the music on the sound system to a slower song, New Orleans R & B.*]

SISSY NA NA [to KRISTA, *away from other guests*]: You listen here. He had nothing for you then, and he's got nothing for you now.

KRISTA: We're older now, we can talk, we can be friends.

[KRISTA *tries to get away.* SISSY NA NA *holds her close.*]

SISSY NA NA: Krista, look at me, *look*.

KRISTA: What?

SISSY NA NA: There is a woman in there that you are afraid to look at. A woman who accepts gifts. A woman who plans for the future. A woman who gives and receives love. A woman who stands tall, on solid ground. Bait Boy will not help you find that woman.

KRISTA: She's not there.

SISSY NA NA: You've never looked.

KRISTA: Because I can't.

SISSY NA NA [*indicating "don't tell me that"*]: Uh-uh.

KRISTA: My daddy told me people don't change.

SISSY NA NA: Yeah, and what was your daddy doing to you when he told you that? Well?

KRISTA: You suck, Sissy.

SISSY NA NA: Your daddy was not interested in being a role model for you.

[KRISTA *runs toward* BAIT BOY.]

Krista, I am trying to give you a gift here. Krista, can't you just take it? Just take it, it's right here!

KRISTA: *Bait Boy!* You *were* legendary.

BAIT BOY: Thank you, baby!

KRISTA: You would work the crowd at Cat's straight through till morning! Doing handstands and shit, bringing girls up on stage to monkey on a stick.

BAIT BOY: I originated that, bringing girls up on stage to dance.

FRANCIS [*slow dancing with one or two female* PARTY GUESTS]: Men have been bringing girls up on stage to dance since the beginning of time.

KRISTA: And then you started asking me up there to dance. I was eighteen years old.

BAIT BOY: You were. And you could dance.

FRANCIS: Everybody dance . . .

[KRISTA, BAIT BOY, FRANCIS, *and some* PARTY GUESTS *dance for a couple minutes. It is not wild; it is like silly couples dancing, switching partners, that sort of thing. It is possible they get* WAYNE *involved. At some point,* KRISTA *and* BAIT BOY *slip off and dance solo on the stairs or balcony.* TANYA *has been watching* ZOE *from across the party. Now, she stands next to her, watching* ZOE *type on her iPad.*]

TANYA [*to* ZOE]: So this is for some blog?

ZOE: No, it's a paper. Well, more like a portrait, actually.

TANYA: A portrait of us?

ZOE: Yes.

TANYA: Well, what do you see when you look at me?

ZOE: Well, I see a woman . . .

TANYA: Okay.

ZOE: A woman with a nice long neck.

TANYA [*kind of covering it*]: Oh God.

ZOE: No, no don't.

[ZOE *reaches out and moves* TANYA's *hand. Maybe she keeps holding it?*]

A woman who . . . has seen a lot of things and come to terms with them. Maybe some sadness?

[TANYA *is like, "well."*]

But a lot of caring, like here, I see that here—

[ZOE *indicates* TANYA's *cheekbones.*]

And . . . smart. I think you're smart.

TANYA: Well, you know I barely went to college.

ZOE: Did you dance for Miss Ruby?

TANYA: Oh God no. That was not my area of expertise. It was hard to get hired in her club, you had to audition, and there were all these minimum requirements . . .

ZOE: But you work in the Quarter?

TANYA: I do. Sometimes.

ZOE: And you live here?

TANYA: Right up there. For ten years.

ZOE: Do you think I could see your room?

TANYA: Today is not a good day for that, sugar.

ZOE: Where *do* you work?

TANYA: Baby, all these questions! Ya gotta soak it in.

ZOE: But don't you think, if you just soak it in all the time, you wind up . . .

TANYA: Lost, like us?

ZOE: No, I didn't mean—

TANYA: Well, that's the gamble. You can repress everything and be miserable one way, or you can release yourself into the primal moment and be miserable in another.

ZOE: But wait. That's not a gamble, because you're miserable both ways.

[TANYA *reaches out and puts her hand above* ZOE's *head as though she is sprinkling magic fairy dust on* ZOE's *head.*]

TANYA: So pretty.

ZOE: Are you okay?

TANYA: Yeah, sure. I'm just thinking about somebody else.

[TANYA *leaves* ZOE, *walks up the steps and into her room. At the same time.* WAYNE *changes the music to something livelier, something in the world of Rebirth Brass Band or the Meter or Jesse Hill's Ooh Poo Pah Doo, with the guests calling and responding to the song. If they do, the following lines should come in the gaps between sung lines.*]

BAIT BOY [*to* ZOE]: So what do you think about all this, kid—

ZOE: You know I hate it / when you call me that!

BAIT BOY: —I mean, what do you think about all this, Zoe?

ZOE: I think this is the realest place I've ever been.

[FRANCIS, WAYNE, *and* ZOE *all kind of high-five and laugh.* FRANCIS *starts dancing with* ZOE.]

BAIT BOY: Hey, watch it, Frannie.

ZOE: Can I come live with you guys?

FRANCIS [*jokingly pulling* ZOE *toward a room*]: Sure baby, we got a room for you right here.

[ZOE *is cracking up and pulling away—she knows how to handle this, almost.*]

WAYNE: Horndog.

BAIT BOY: Frannie, *yo.*

[SHADY CHARACTER TWO *from the Problem Room is filling multiple cups with beer from the keg.*]

SISSY NA NA: Hey, hey, who are you? You know Miss Ruby?

SHADY CHARACTER TWO: Uhh . . .

SISSY NA NA: That's what I thought, you have no idea what's going on, can you please—

[SHADY CHARACTER TWO *throws a beer at* SISSY NA NA.]

Wayne!

WAYNE [*ushering* SHADY CHARACTER TWO *back toward the Problem Room*]: Hey, private party, private party, come on . . .

SISSY NA NA [*yelling to the* PARTY GUESTS]: Can't anybody see we are trying to take care of a community here?!

[*Maybe, like, some cheers and dancing? Like people don't quite get what* SISSY NA NA *is saying?*]

Where's Tanya, we gotta do this now!

[SISSY NA NA *makes her way to* TANYA's *room.*]

ZOE [*dancing with* PARTY GUESTS *and* FRANCIS]: You guys know, right, you guys know this is, like, impossible to describe?

FRANCIS: Try to grab it and—it's gone.

ZOE: On Instagram whatever . . . it's all just happening.

FRANCIS: Let it happen!

ZOE: Do you know how much I have to squeeze into every day so I can get into college? Student council, young entrepreneurs, the newspaper—I wake up every morning with a . . . a . . . a gorilla sitting on my chest.

FRANCIS: Huh?

WAYNE: Go easy, kid.

ZOE: I'm not a kid!

WAYNE [*laughing*]: Baby, you're sixteen!

FRANCIS [*almost seeing following as a potential line of poetry*]: Invite the gorilla up on to your chest.

ZOE: I wanna live at the Hummingbird Hotel!

[*Cheers and dancing.*]

WAYNE [*to* ZOE]: Yeah you rite! I know every inch of this place, every duct-taped pipe, every champagne-stained wall . . .

FRANCIS: This is your domain!

WAYNE: This is my kingdom!

BAIT BOY: King Wayne!

[BAIT BOY *tosses* WAYNE *a plastic crown that someone was wearing as a party hat. Everyone cheers.* SISSY NA NA *pulls* TANYA *out of her room.*]

SISSY NA NA: Come on.

TANYA: All right. So first we'll do the girls' song—

SISSY NA NA: Tanya, no.

TANYA: And then we'll do memories—

WAYNE [*to the crowd, very big, suddenly Shakespearian*]: This is where we live! No one can take it from us! No one can drive us out!

[*More cheering.*]

SISSY NA NA [*to* TANYA]: Look, let's just get her down first and see how she does.

[SISSY NA NA *goes to check on* MISS RUBY.]

WAYNE [*to the crowd*]: All this is ours!

[WAYNE *looks out over his kingdom, as though it is a vast estate that runs on for miles.*]

PARTY GUESTS, FRANCIS, ZOE, AND BAIT BOY [*chanting*]: King Wayne, King, Wayne, King Wayne.

[TANYA *runs down to* WAYNE.]

TANYA: Wayne! We're going to bring her down, are you ready? Wayne—now!

WAYNE [*responding to* TANYA]: What? Oh, okay.

[WAYNE *takes off the party crown.*]

Ah, my kingdom . . .

[TANYA *rubs her face.* SISSY NA NA *comes out of* MISS RUBY's *room.*]

SISSY NA NA: I'm sorry, Tanya.

TANYA [*remembering, panicking*]: Oh God! We have to pass out the—

[SISSY NA NA *points to* FRANCIS, *who is diligently passing out paper ducks.*]

SISSY NA NA: Francis has got it, look.

[SISSY NA NA *heads upstairs with* WAYNE *and* TERRY.]

TANYA [*announcing*]: All right, everyone, we're going to bring her down, let's settle down, keep the stairs clear, and this area too . . .

[*Everyone starts to quiet down.* MISS RUBY's *door opens and* SISSY NA NA *and* WAYNE *back out, carrying some kind of gurney or hospital bed.* TANYA *sees them.*]

TANYA: Okay, here we go!

[TERRY *and a* PARTY GUEST *help carry the bed.* MISS RUBY *is revealed, swaddled in blankets and sheets, her head resting comfortably on pillows. At the moment her eyes are closed; she might as well be a corpse. She is old, very old. Her hair is concealed under a wrap or a shower cap with a flower affixed to it. She is wearing makeup—generous amounts of rouge and eye shadow—and she has a sparkly pink flower tucked behind one ear.* SISSY NA NA *and* WAYNE *struggle to get the bed down the walkway and then to the stairs. They begin to descend the stairs. Everyone is silent and kind of tense because of the difficulty of this maneuver.*]

FRANCIS [*softly, to* KRISTA*?*]: Oh good, they put her makeup on.

TANYA [*softly*]: She looks wonderful, wonderful.

[SISSY NA NA *or* WAYNE *stumbles, maybe descending a few stairs just a little quicker. The crowd gasps.*]

TANYA:	KRISTA:	FRANCIS:
Oh, my lord.	Is she okay?	Watch it, watch it.

WAYNE: We got it, we got it.

[MISS RUBY's *eyes pop open. They continue, with the entire party breathing a bit of a sigh of relief when they get to the ground level. They position* MISS RUBY *near the food. When she is set,* TANYA, KRISTA, BAIT BOY, TERRY, WAYNE, *and* SISSY NA NA *gather close, and the other* PARTY GUESTS *move in just a little.*]

TANYA: Hey, Miss Ruby.

MISS RUBY: Hey, my beautiful girl.

KRISTA: Hi Ru Ru.

[MISS RUBY *turns her head and looks at* KRISTA.]

MISS RUBY: Oh my heavens, Sharon is that you?

[*Everyone kind of looks at* KRISTA.]

KRISTA: No, no Miss Ruby, that's my mama. She passed away, remember? It's Krista, Sharon's daughter.

MISS RUBY: Oh of course, of course. I don't know what happened to
my head, I think I must have hung it on the costume rack back at
the club.

SISSY NA NA: It's okay Miss Ruby, look, all these nice people have
gathered here to tell you good-bye.

[MISS RUBY *looks around.*]

MISS RUBY: Oh my, am I . . . am I . . . ?

TANYA: Yes?

MISS RUBY: Am I in a parking lot?

[*It is hard for those closest to her not to crack up, but they manage to
hold it in.*]

TANYA: Yes, we brought you outside so everyone could say hello. You
are in the parking lot of the Hummingbird Hotel.

MISS RUBY: Oh, well so I am. Home sweet home.

SISSY NA NA: That's right.

MISS RUBY: Well, why don't you wheel me around to the pool? And
ask Georgie to make me a cosmopolitan. The weather's so nice, we
should all go for a swim!

TANYA [*smiling, and kind of telling everyone to wait, they might as
well lie to her*]: Sure, we'll do that in just a bit.

MISS RUBY: In the nude! What the heck. We're all friends here.

FRANCIS [*to the party*]: What do y'all say, should we all go skinny-dipping with Miss Ruby?

[*Everyone cheers.*]

MISS RUBY: My goodness, who are all these people?

TANYA: We gathered everyone together for your funeral.

MISS RUBY: For my what?

SISSY NA NA: For your funeral, remember?

MISS RUBY: Am I dead?

TANYA: No, *no* Miss Ruby— remember? You asked us to have your funeral before you died so you could hear all the nice things that people had to say about you.

MISS RUBY: I said that?

SISSY NA NA: You did, Miss Ruby.

MISS RUBY: But I'm not going to die.

FRANCIS [*to no one and everyone*]: See? She's immortal, I'm telling you.

TANYA: That's my girl!

MISS RUBY: You know what I always say—the show must go on! My mother says I've been saying that since I was twelve. Because people need to keep their hands busy; if not, they are going to wind up with the wrong thing in their hand—the wrong pipe, the wrong woman's behind. And if you don't have a job, you might as well put on a show. Look at this, they keep up this place so nice, don't they? I just love the pink walls.

WAYNE: Aren't they pretty, Miss Ruby?

MISS RUBY: Wayne Patrick Murphy, is that you?

WAYNE: It's me, Miss Ruby.

MISS RUBY: But you got fat!

WAYNE: I did, Miss Ruby.

MISS RUBY: You were such a scrawny little teenager, what happened to you?

WAYNE: I drank a lot of beer, Miss Ruby.

MISS RUBY: You see? You should have been putting on a show!

WAYNE: Nobody would want to see my show, Miss Ruby.

MISS RUBY: I've always tried to imagine all of you as little yellow baby ducks.

[*Does everyone wave the paper ducks?*]

Even when you came to me with your coke nosebleeds, or the goddamn ring that you stole from your uncle's wife, who didn't need it anyway, but you felt guilty and I would look at—

[*She points to* BAIT BOY.]

—*you*, a little baby duck with a ring in its beak, and say, *take it back*, and you'd say, *but he'll never understand*, and I would say, *take it back, now*. And you would ruffle your yellow feathers and swim away.

BAIT BOY: I came back, Miss Ruby.

MISS RUBY: I think I read that when baby ducks are born, their sex is not yet determined, that *that* part comes later. And so I imagine you all as little tiny puffy bright-yellow nongendered baby ducks . . . That's what you are . . .

[MISS RUBY *falls asleep. For a moment we hear her light snore.*]

WAYNE: Did she just fall asleep?

[*As the following conversation starts, everyone relaxes a little, with some heading to the keg and others talking among themselves, resting their paper ducks in their hats or on their shoulders for a few minutes.*]

TANYA: That's what happens—
she's in and out.

FRANCIS: See, I told you she
didn't want a funeral.

SISSY NA NA: It's too much for
her, too much stimulus.

KRISTA: I don't look anything like
my mother.

BAIT BOY: Y'all look alike when
you're sad.

KRISTA: Oh great.

TANYA [*announcing*]: So, when
she comes to, we're going to
jump right to the final song.
Everybody stay close so we
can be ready to start, and
don't get too drunk.

FRANCIS: She didn't want a
funeral . . .

TANYA: Francis, help me pick up trash. I want things to be in order when she wakes up.

[FRANCIS *starts to help, maybe picking up a couple cups.*]

FRANCIS: I mean, she's blind or whatever, right?

[TANYA *grabs a garbage bag and starts collecting trash, avoiding* MISS RUBY *on her bed.* FRANCIS *helps* TANYA *for a minute, before drifting off to observe* MISS RUBY *from a distance.* WAYNE *keeps an eye on* TANYA.]

ZOE: Is it okay if I . . .

SISSY NA NA: Sure baby, sure, you should see this.

KRISTA [*to* BAIT BOY]: Come smoke a joint with me. For old times' sake. *Come on.*

[KRISTA *and* BAIT BOY *move to the edge of the parking lot, or up on the balcony.*]

TERRY: This is a good woman.

SISSY NA NA: Yes, indeed.

TERRY: I may not be perfect, but if it wasn't for her, I'd be dead.

SISSY NA NA: Tell her.

TERRY: Miss Ruby, if it wasn't for you, I'd be dead. You're the one who took the gun out of my hand and locked it up in your drawer. You're the one who would buy me a new shirt for every week I stayed off the horse—

SISSY NA NA: They weren't new, they belonged to her son—

TERRY: I know, but they were new to me.

SISSY NA NA [*to* ZOE]: She called them resurrection shirts.

TERRY: You told me the dirtiest jokes I ever heard in all my days. The thing about you, Miss Ruby, you never asked me to change. You just knew. You knew there was something decent under all this muck. And you helped me remember that too.

ZOE: I'm glad I got to meet you, Miss Ruby.

KRISTA: How were we together for six years and never . . .

BAIT BOY: Never what?

KRISTA: I don't know. Buy a house. Make a baby.

BAIT BOY: Well, we almost did.

KRISTA [*referring to a miscarriage*]: I know and then . . . that was a terrible day, when that happened.

BAIT BOY: It wasn't meant to be. I mean, you were twenty-one when that happened.

KRISTA: That's old enough.

BAIT BOY: Yeah, yeah, but I mean, where were we living then?

KRISTA: It was before we moved here, we were . . . we were in Jackie's place.

[*They both remember how shitty that flophouse was.*]

BAIT BOY: It wasn't meant to be.

[FRANCIS *comes up to* ZOE.]

ZOE: She's the real deal.

FRANCIS: Poetry is everywhere. I'm just the editor. Hey, look . . . instead of college, try this . . .

[FRANCIS *hands* ZOE *a handmade book.*]

ZOE: This is your poetry?

FRANCIS: Free of charge . . .

[FRANCIS *backs away.*]

[TANYA *has been picking up trash, but at some point she gets lost in thought and is just standing there, in the middle of the party, maybe holding some Solo cups in one hand and dirty paper plates in another.* WAYNE *sees her: he knows that distant look.*]

WAYNE: Hey. Hey.

TANYA: I just want *one.*

WAYNE [*re: the plates*]: Come on, give me that.

TANYA: I know you know I had old ones hidden in my room, and they're gone, Wayne, you went in there, / you have a key.

WAYNE: I want to show you something, come here, come here.

[WAYNE *walks* TANYA *over toward the old restaurant.*]

BAIT BOY: When we're seventy, you think you and me will be able to be friends?

KRISTA: No.

BAIT BOY: Come on. The two of us, smoking big fat doobs on the porch of your house in the country somewhere. Chickens. We're in rocking chairs and shit. Grandkids running around.

KRISTA: Whose grandkids?

BAIT BOY: I don't know. Maybe we can rent some.

WAYNE: See? The old restaurant.

TANYA: Oh God—

WAYNE: Under all those boxes in the storage room is a full bar. Under all the moldy wall-to-wall carpet is a dance floor.

[*They both crack up—they've gotten pretty high pretty fast.*]

[WAYNE *calls to* TERRY.]

Hey Terry you know how to pull up carpet?

TERRY: In my sleep Mr. Wayne.

WAYNE: We can do this, Tanya—we can save the Hummingbird!

TANYA: Save it? What do you mean save it?

KRISTA: 1-800-Rent-a-Grandkid!

[A beat.]

[BAIT BOY and KRISTA laugh and take another hit from the pot. MISS RUBY starts to wake up.]

WAYNE: It's just an expression, baby. I mean . . . we can make it all nice again.

MISS RUBY: Uhh . . . where am I going?

SISSY NA NA: It's okay. sweetie, we gotcha.

[Another beat. WAYNE and TANYA both know that WAYNE isn't telling the whole story, that the Hummingbird is in danger of being sold.]

WAYNE: Come on Tanya, put your confidence on.

[TANYA takes out her lipstick, puts it on.]

BAIT BOY: And I'll buy a giant, like banner and paint a blue sky on it . . . And we can just chill . . .

There ya go.

KRISTA: Where would Joyce live?

TANYA: You know I'm gonna get one somehow, Wayne. They always find me when I need them.

[BAIT BOY whispers in KRISTA's ear. KRISTA cracks up.]

SISSY NA NA: Tanya, she's up, let's do this.

TANYA [*speaking quietly so as not to scare* MISS RUBY]: Okay, everybody—Sissy fix her pillow so she can see—everybody grab hold
of a duck. . . . Ready? Everyone ready?

[*Everybody gathers around. It is hard for* KRISTA *and* BAIT BOY *to stop
laughing, and* ZOE *sees this and is pretty shocked but doesn't really
know what to do about it.* SISSY NA NA *puts her arm around* ZOE *and
stands by her. Everybody is getting in place with their ducks.* SISSY
NA NA *starts the song. Everyone is singing, and it is sweet but totally
off-key and not entirely confident. But everyone is giving it their best
shot. The core group of friends begin walking around* MISS RUBY's
*bed with the paper ducks so that the ducks are swimming in a circle,
perhaps held over everyone's heads? Up on the balcony, people make a
train of ducks as well.* MISS RUBY's *eyes are wide with delight.*]

ALL:
> Just a closer walk with thee.
> Grant it, Ruby.
> If you please.
> Daily walking next to thee.
> Let it be, Ruby, let it be.

TANYA:
> See, Miss Ruby? Just like the old days . . .

ALL:
> I am weak, but thou art strong.
> Keep me, Ruby, from all harm.

FRANCIS:
> Look at us fools, remarkable!

ALL:
> I'll be satisfied as long
> As I walk, let me walk close to thee.

KRISTA:

I wonder what she hears?

[*The moment* KRISTA *says the above line, the lights shift to focus on* MISS RUBY *and her angelic face, and the singing shifts so that it sounds like a chorus of angels—gorgeous, ever-shifting harmonies. Perhaps the exterior walls of the Hummingbird now look bright pink. Perhaps the ducks now float magically through the dim light, glowing a little.* MISS RUBY *speaks as her younger self.*]

MISS RUBY:

And in the beginning there was *sex.*

I believe the sexual act was first imagined as energy, as energy creating energy.

If there *is* a God, and if God imagined sex, the impulse came from inside—and had nowhere to go.

And so I see this lonely God, sitting on a solitary cloud, desperately desiring the feeling of being *with.*

In the burlesque club of my dreams, there's no *he* paying for *she* performing for *him* who is mad at *her*—we are all in the room *with* each other, open and unafraid, reveling in the present moment together.

This is ecstatic experience! Can you imagine? If this could happen?

Why do you all fuck up so bad all the time?

Don't you start telling me about how *some* people get to have more fuckups than others, because of the fancy last names they were born into.

It's true. You've drawn the short end of the stick.

But you are seekers who have been drawn here, to the edges of the world. And you hold the potential to teach the world something about itself. You live in a city that reveres the ecstatic moment. How do you live inside this ecstasy and still use it? Carry it with you without being utterly consumed?

There is nothing more I can do for you now. I am in the last ten hours of my life. Did I live my life right? Did I not realize what my life had become until I was in the middle of it? Did I regret that I did not have enough money to send my son to a good college, which led to him serving in the military and serving for nineteen years before getting shot through the head by a sniper in Iraq?

We are who we are. And you are the most gorgeous group of fuckups I've ever seen.

[MISS RUBY *lies back. She is back in this time.* TANYA *approaches* MISS RUBY, *takes her hand.*]

TANYA: Sweetie, your hands are cold . . .

[TANYA *puts* MISS RUBY'*s hands underneath the blankets. Then* TANYA'*s hands emerge holding a bottle of pain pills.*]

MISS RUBY: Those are mine.

[TANYA *opens the bottle of pills.*]

Tanya, *don't.*

[TANYA *shakes a pill out onto her hand.*]

Don't run from your ragged self. Be *with* it. Be *with* each other. Be *with* this moment that is slipping through our fingers as I speak . . .

[TANYA *takes the pill.*]

[*It's like opening Pandora's box. The party shifts down, down, down to a particularly nasty gear.*]

[*Cut to three hours later.* KRISTA *and* BAIT BOY *are dirty dancing— maybe not making out, but they might as well be.* TANYA *is wandering around the stage in her own world—she is probably four or five pain pills under by now.* MISS RUBY *is still downstairs—maybe there is a* PARTY GUEST *with her, paying respects.* SISSY NA NA *enters with plastic bags filled with chips from the minimarket down the street.* WAYNE *is hanging with* TERRY, *and he is totally pissed at* TANYA *for having gotten high, which probably means he's downed a couple more beers out of spite.* ZOE *is chanting with* FRANCIS—*she hasn't really seen yet what is going on with* BAIT BOY *and* KRISTA. *She echoes and overlaps the following chant, until she notices* BAIT BOY *and* KRISTA.]

ZOE AND FRANCIS:
>   *We are the damned!*
>   *We are the damned!*
>   *We will be broken!*
>   *And realigned!*
>   *Maybe none of this was meant to stand!*

[ZOE *and* FRANCIS *repeat this chant over the following dialogue, until indicated. As* TANYA *speaks, she ascends the staircase and works to pull her bra off from under her dress.*]

TANYA: Hey Krista—

Hey Krista—

Hey Krista—

Hey Krista, do you want to
see my strip routine?

SISSY NA NA [*referring to* MISS
RUBY]: Wayne, she's still

Hey Wayne—

Hey Wayne—

Hey Wayne—

Hey Wayne, do you want to see my strip routine?

Hey Sissy, do you want to see my strip routine?

[TANYA *pulls her bra out from under her dress and twirls it over her head.*]

[TANYA *is throwing herself at a male* PARTY GUEST *on the balcony.* WAYNE *is climbing the stairs to catch her.*]

down here? I asked you to take her up an hour ago!

WAYNE: I thought Terry and Bait Boy—

SISSY NA NA: *Forget it*, Wayne, I'll just do it myself. Tanya, can you—

[*referring to* TANYA]: Oh, fucking fabulous.

[ZOE *stops chanting and grabs* FRANCIS's *arm, pointing at* KRISTA *and* BAIT BOY.]

ZOE: Hey, hey—

FRANCIS: Oh yeah, that's not good—hold on.

[FRANCIS *is trying to break up* KRISTA *and* BAIT BOY.]

FRANCIS: Hey, hey, come on you two, that's enough.

ZOE: Greg!

BAIT BOY: Don't worry about it, Zoe, it's okay.

FRANCIS: This is not cool.

BAIT BOY: It's okay.

FRANCIS: Come on, she's your kid.

BAIT BOY: She's not my *kid!*

[BAIT BOY *pushes* ZOE *to the ground, hard.*]

FRANCIS: Dude—

ZOE: Ow.

BAIT BOY: Oh shit.

SISSY NA NA: Classy, Bait Boy, just like always.

[SISSY NA NA *goes over to* ZOE.]

TANYA [*to the* PARTY GUESTS]: I tried out to dance for Miss Ruby, but I couldn't do the splits or the backbends— which were the minimum requirement . . .

Come on, come sit by Miss Ruby. Wayne, *Wayne!*

[*Referring to* TANYA]

[TANYA *throws one of her shoes at* WAYNE.]

Wayne, will you catch her?

Stay away, Wayne!

[SISSY NA NA *puts* ZOE *in a chair by* MISS RUBY; ZOE *holds* MISS RUBY's *hand.*]

KRISTA: Come on, Bait Boy, let's get out of here.

BAIT BOY: Get away from me! *You* did this!

KRISTA: Me?

BAIT BOY: Every time I get my shit together, *you* come along and fuck it all up.

KRISTA: No, no no—

BAIT BOY: You keep dragging me down. *I was legendary!*

KRISTA: You were not legendary. You were a fucked-up guy whose job was to keep the party going at a karaoke bar on Bourbon Street. A guy who *acted* like he was famous while he tried to fuck every little seventeen-year-old.

BAIT BOY: I don't MESS with *underage* girls!

[TANYA *takes off her underwear and twirls it over her head. Perhaps* WAYNE *tries to catch her, but she ducks under his arm and runs past him, laughing and throwing her underwear into the crowd.*]

KRISTA: Oh, pardon me, every eighteen-, nineteen-year-old that would walk into the club.

[KRISTA *runs to* ZOE *and grabs her by the shoulders, speaking to her directly.*]

This is what I am *talking about here*, Zoe. There is *real shit* that goes down in life,

139

and there is *real shit* that he will *pull on you* if you're not careful. Do not *trust him,* little girl: he *knows what he is doing,* you hear me?

BAIT BOY: Zoe, no, don't listen to her bullshit!

WAYNE: Tanya, stop! You are not going to take off your dress and throw it into the crowd. You are not going to take your tits in your hand and pretend like you are squirting them at everybody!

TANYA: Come on, Wayne, it's fun!

[*Perhaps* TANYA *runs into* MISS RUBY's *room, and* WAYNE *follows her.*]

[*There is a skirmish where* SISSY NA NA *tries to separate* KRISTA, ZOE, *and* BAIT BOY.]

BAIT BOY: What about you, Krista? What about your fucking abuse history that you *refused to face?*

KRISTA: No, not this, not now—

BAIT BOY: You talked to me *exactly twice* about the fucked-up shit that happened to you when you were nine.

KRISTA: Why are you doing this?

BAIT BOY: *Twice in ten years, because you are damaged beyond all hope, Krista, and you know it, you know it!*

[TERRY *has been watching and somehow trips* BAIT BOY *and gets him into some kind of headlock, maybe on the ground?*]

TERRY: You don't know nothing about hope. Nothing about love. Nothing about anything except the lie that is your sorry-ass self.

[BAIT BOY *struggles against* TERRY*'s grip.*]

WAYNE: You are not going to go running around rubbing your naked body on people you do not know and you are not going to start listing the names of the three children you gave away between the ages of eighteen and thirty five!

[KRISTA *grabs* TERRY*'s hand.*]

KRISTA: Come on, Terry, come build me a house.

[KRISTA *pulls* TERRY *aside to a corner, trying to make out with him.*]

TERRY: Baby, no.

KRISTA: Come on, I'm begging you for it.

[TANYA *opens the door. There are two staging options. One: She is completely naked and descends the stairs. Two: She still has her*

[KRISTA *drops to her knees, starts unbuckling his pants.*]

dress on, runs out of the room, tries to pull off her dress, and WAYNE *stops her.*]

TANYA [*to everyone, as a kind of announcement*]: What are you all afraid of? Don't you ever want to lay it all bare? Sometimes I just wanna say, here I am. Here I am. Here I am.

TERRY: Not like this. Stop. Be here. Be still.

[TERRY *pulls* KRISTA *to her feet, calms her down, holds her close.*]

[*A moment passes.* TANYA's *announcement has landed solidly on everyone at the Hummingbird.*]

BAIT BOY: Y'all are fucking pitiful. Y'all were born to be stuck right fucking here. Not me, 'cause I knew how to keep my eyes open, how to watch for the helicopter that was going to lift me out of here. And I know you will bad-mouth me until the day I die for getting out, for being airlifted out, and guess what—I don't give a flying fuck. Because my head is clear, my head is held high in Atlanta, and it's true, I live in a real nice house that I did not buy, I do not own, but I do my fair share, I do the dishes, I fix the ceiling fan, I built Zoe a bookshelf, didn't I, Zoe? I participate in the household, and that is what you call sweat equity. Which is something y'all bitches don't know nothin' about. The only equity y'all know about is beg, borrowed, or stolen. But I got new eyes now, and I know how to succeed in my life, no thanks to all you bitches.

Come on, Zoe, we're getting out of this shit hole.

MISS RUBY: Gregory.

[BAIT BOY *stops. For a moment,* MISS RUBY *is very lucid.*]

You have been running since you walked through my door at seventeen, hungry, with a sprained ankle and one backpack to your name. And you will keep running until you face whatever it is that makes you feel so unloved.

BAIT BOY: Come on, Zoe, *come on.*

[BAIT BOY *leaves. Maybe* ZOE *takes off her tutu. Maybe* FRANCIS *picks up the book of poetry that has fallen to the ground and hands it to* ZOE. *And she leaves.*]

FRANCIS: Jesus, he always did know how to spoil a party.

MISS RUBY: Charlie? *Charlie? Charlie, where are you?*

[MISS RUBY *continues to call for Charlie.*]

SISSY NA NA: Here we go . . .

TANYA: It never ends.

[KRISTA *wriggles out of* TERRY's *arms. They face each other.*]

TERRY: Hey, hey. It's okay.

WAYNE [*to* TANYA]: I know, I know.

[TANYA *collapses to the ground.* WAYNE *tries awkwardly to comfort her.* TERRY *tries to make a move toward* KRISTA. *She backs away defensively.*]

SISSY NA NA [*taking* MISS RUBY's *hand*]: Here I am, Mama.

[MISS RUBY *is quiet.*]

TERRY [*to* KRISTA]: It's called tenderness. It's all that I own in the world.

MISS RUBY: Oh Charlie, thank goodness. I thought you were gone for good.

SISSY NA NA: No, Mama, it's me. I'm right here. I'm home.

[KRISTA *runs away.* SISSY NA NA *comforts* MISS RUBY.]

SCENE 2

[*The lights shift to dawn light as the characters drift offstage or into new positions. It's dawn again, 5:45 A.M.* TERRY, *still in his wig and hula skirt, sleeps leaning up against the wall of the hotel near* WAYNE's *office. No one else is visible. A light features* ZOE. *She is in her class. She swishes open her iPad. As* ZOE *speaks,* KRISTA *wanders back on stage from the street and sits in a broken chair or something.*]

ZOE: I don't know why I got to be born into this body, in a hospital, in relative comfort, in Atlanta. But I don't take that accident for granted.

[FRANCIS *sits up in the backseat of the abandoned car. He is totally hungover, still drunk from yesterday. He groans and tumbles out of the car, looks toward the office.*]

It's nearly impossible to track down the people I met that day: if you Google any of their names, the best you can hope for is an arrest report, or a list of poets reading at a bar on a Sunday afternoon.

FRANCIS: He made coffee yet?

KRISTA: No.

FRANCIS: Shit. I gotta work today.

ZOE: If you race by them on the street, they'll be invisible to you . . .

FRANCIS: Hey, you think I could maybe use your shower?

KRISTA: I don't have a room here anymore.

FRANCIS: Oh, right. Shit.

ZOE: But if you pause and look one of them in the eye, they will take you by the hand and lead you down a rabbit hole . . .

[FRANCIS *is at the keg.*]

FRANCIS: Wow. Still cold.

ZOE: Into a moment that's messy and honest and real.

[FRANCIS *looks at the keg.*]

FRANCIS: Well. When in Rome . . .

[FRANCIS *finds a cup on the ground and pours himself a beer.*]

KRISTA: Francis, I don't live anywhere.

FRANCIS: Aw, come on, baby. You live right here.

[FRANCIS *taps his heart.*]

ZOE: Bait Boy—Greg—disappeared from our house three days after our trip. Completely evaporated. My mom was crushed. I was ambivalent.

[SISSY NA NA *comes out of* MISS RUBY's *room—she's carefully containing panic and emotion.*]

SISSY NA NA: Guys, I think it's happening. Get up to her room if you want to be there.

[KRISTA *runs toward the office.* SISSY NA NA *goes and knocks on* TANYA's *door.*]

KRISTA: Wayne!

[KRISTA *enters the back room of the office, where* WAYNE *sleeps.*]

ZOE: Since then, I've been trying to embrace the incoherence of it all. Celebrate it, actually.

SISSY NA NA: Tanya. Tanya. Tanya.

[TANYA *does not answer.* SISSY NA NA *speaks to* FRANCIS, *pointing to sleeping* TERRY.]

Get him up.

ZOE: It's only been a few weeks, and already it's beginning to fade from my mind . . .

FRANCIS: Hey. Terry.

[FRANCIS *goes to* TERRY. KRISTA *and* WAYNE *emerge from the office.*]

SISSY NA NA [*to* WAYNE]: Where's Tanya?

[WAYNE's *head falls into his hands.*]

WAYNE: Oh, no.

[WAYNE *walks to the door of the Problem Room.* KRISTA *is helping* TERRY *stand up.*]

KRISTA: Come on, let me help you up . . .

ZOE: The idiosyncrasies, the remarkable contradictions . . .

[WAYNE *knocks on the door of the Problem Room. The door opens.* KRISTA *takes the wig off* TERRY's *head. They walk up the stairs.*]

WAYNE: I need her.

ZOE: That remind me of the same things in myself . . .

[TANYA *emerges from the Problem Room.*]

WAYNE: Come on, it's time.

TANYA: Oh God . . .

WAYNE: I know. Take a deep breath.

[*Everyone but* FRANCIS *heads into* MISS RUBY's *room.* ZOE *disappears. As* WAYNE *and* TANYA *ascend the stairs,* TANYA *speaks.*]

TANYA: I'm sorry. I'm so sorry. I'm sorry. Here we go, here we go. This is it.

SISSY NA NA: Francis, you coming?

[SISSY NA NA *goes in and closes the door.*]

FRANCIS:
    Serpentine echoes reverberate
    In mind's eye
    Stepping-stones across a river
    Of minutes, hours, days, decades, centuries

Memory working out
Now's version of then

Her voice
Up from the dirt
Unencumbered
Undenied.

And here we are
Confluence of saints and devils
in the early dawn.

Sometimes a strange gem
Falls into your hand

Steal what you see
This is the place

[SISSY NA NA *opens the door to* MISS RUBY's *room and comes out onto the balcony.*]

SISSY NA NA [*to* FRANCIS]: Come on, baby. Last call.

[SISSY NA NA *goes back into* MISS RUBY's *room and closes the door. We can vaguely see* SISSY NA NA *and the others around* MISS RUBY's *bed, behind the blinds.* FRANCIS *watches the sunrise as the lights in the theater black out.*]